# A Pictorial History of Radio

# Books by Irving Settel

Effective Retail Advertising
The Ad-Viser
Television Advertising & Production Handbook
Top TV Shows of the Year
Best Television Humor of 1956
Best Television Humor of 1957
Great Television Sermons
How to Write Television Comedy
The Best of Armstrong Circle Theatre
A Pictorial History of Radio

# A Pictorial History of RADIO

*by* IRVING SETTEL

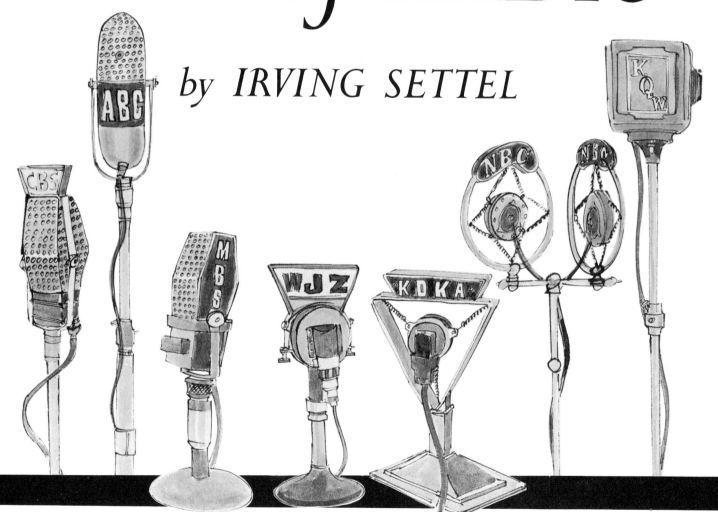

GROSSET & DUNLAP · PUBLISHERS · NEW YORK

# Picture Credits

Photographs, engravings, drawings, and other illustrations in this book, unless otherwise specifically credited below, are used through the courtesy of the following organizations:

New York Public Library; American Museum of Natural History; Western Union Telegraph Company; New York Telephone Company; American Telephone and Telegraph Company; Radio Corporation of America; *Television Age* Magazine; Radio Station KDKA; *Broadcasting* Magazine; National Broadcasting Company; Westinghouse Company; Columbia Broadcasting System; American Broadcasting Company; Bell Telephone Laboratories; General Electric Company; Allen B. Du Mont Laboratories; WOR-Mutual Broadcasting System; Philco Corporation; Hartwest Productions, Inc.; Radio Station WHOM; Radio Station WNEW; Radio Station WMCA; United States Navy; United States Army; and the Educational Television and Radio Center.

Credit for many of the photographs go to the following individuals:

Thomas Cook Knight; Rosenfeld; F. A. Schultz; Aiklee; Harold Stein; Robert Perkins; Matthews; Eileen Darbl; Gary Wagner; Walt David; J. Peter Happel; Archie Lieberman; George Harris; Robert Phillips; Vernon Merritt III—Black Star; T. C. Rapoport—*Saturday Evening Post;* Bill Mitchell; and Joseph G. Chenoweth.

In addition, the following firms supplied photographs:

BROWN BROTHERS
Pages 68, *left and right;* 69; 73; 77.

CULVER PICTURES
Pages 51, *left;* 72, *lower right;* 74, *upper left;* 75, *right;* 76, *lower right;* 83, *lower right;* 95, *upper left, lower right;* 104, *bottom;* 117; 118, *top;* 129, *right;* 133, *left;* 134, *top right and left;* 135, *top and bottom;* 136, *all pictures;* 144, *right;* 149, *top and bottom;* 150, *upper right;* 152, *upper right.*

WIDE WORLD
Pages 60, *top and bottom;* 104, *top.*

*For Mom and Jules*

# Acknowledgments

Without the encouragement, advice and assistance of many persons, this book could never have come into being and the author wishes to acknowledge his deep appreciation for this help. Deserving special mention are the staffs of the national broadcasting networks, who opened their files and made available to the author many of the priceless photographs contained herein.

The author is specifically indebted to Walter (Izzy) Siegal, Manager of the Photographic Department of the Columbia Broadcasting System, who generously gave time from his very busy schedule to assist the author in the selection of photographs and in formulating many of the captions. Also of CBS, the author wishes to thank the staff of the Photographic Department; Bill Ackerman, who provided a great number of wonderful pictures, Charles J. Oppenheim, Larry Loewenstein, Robert J. Dunne of the Legal Department, Mel Spiegel, Irving Gitlin, Dorothy Leffler, and Charles Steinberg.

The author also wishes to thank members of the staff at the National Broadcasting Company, including Kenneth Bilby, John Porter, Sid Desfore, Bob Eno and Jack Tracy. Also deserving the gratitude of the author are the staff members of the American Broadcasting Company, including Mike Foster, Hank Warner, Tony Leighton and Tony Egan.

Further, the author is greatly indebted to the following persons for their generous assistance and valuable contributions of both pictures and text for this book: Harold Gold of the Mutual Broadcasting System; Orrin E. Dunlap, Jr. and Raymond P. Descalzi of the Radio Corporation of America; Mr. Sol Taishoff, Editor and Publisher of *Broadcasting and Telecasting* Magazine, and Frances Pelzman; Art King of *Television Age;* Jean Drechsler of KDKA; Howard Batsford of the New York Telephone Company; M. P. Cosgrove of the American Telegraph & Telegraph Company; Gilbert H. Furgurson of Westinghouse Electric Corporation; Murray D. Kirkwood of the International Telephone and Telegraph Corporation; George P. Oslin of the Western Union Telegraph Company; R. M. Lovell of the General Electric Company; Brooke Alexander of *Fortune* Magazine; Major Ben R. Fern, United States Air Force, chief of the Magazine and Book Branch of the Department of Defense; John G. Trezevant of the National Association of Radio and Television Broadcasters; Gertrude Broderick of the United States Department of Health, Education and Welfare; Abel Green, editor of *Variety;* Layne Beaty, chief of radio and television of the United States Department of Agriculture; Sherril Taylor of the Radio Advertising Bureau; William A. Harper of the Educational Television and Radio Center; Edward W. Allen, Jr., of Allen B. Du Mont Laboratories; Virginia Daiker, Reference Librarian of the Library of Congress; E. T. Buck Harris of the Screen Actors' Guild; Herbert Rosen of Audio Master Corporation; Morris Rosenfeld; Jack Gould, radio and television editor of the *New York Times;* Colonel Bertram Kalisch of the Department of Defense; Lou Frankel of Pulse; H. Lyman Armes of the Department of Commerce.

The author also wishes to thank President Emeritus Robert S. Pace, President Edward J. Mortola, Dean Joseph F. Sinzer, Dr. Jack S. Schiff, and the members of the faculty of Pace College, for their help and encouragement.

Thanks are due too to Arthur Smith of The Citadel Press for many helpful suggestions and many hours of editing and research on this book.

Finally, deserving special mention, is Gertrude Settel, the author's wife, whose untiring assistance in the preparation of the manuscript and whose patience, wisdom and discernment made this book possible.

IRVING SETTEL
*Bayside, N. Y.*

# Contents

# A Lament for Old-time Radio* BY BROCK BROWER

I happened to hear, not long ago, a lecture by the young television director, John Frankenheimer. He talked at length about "the medium," and his remarks, if not always optimistic, were at least highly futuristic. We seemed to be very much in the presence of a soaring comet, some sidereal kin of that pointed star that rotates on *Playhouse 90*, and during the ensuing question period everybody tried to grab its tail. Everybody, that is, except a brave old lady who rose to put the question: "Some of us like to listen to the radio, young man. Why don't you put on some good radio shows like they used to?" The audience laughed uneasily, and Mr. Frankenheimer scratched his head. "I don't know, madam," he said finally, "but I can sure sympathize with you. . . ."

I think I can too. Radio, for me, is part of the Lost Childhood, and those old-time radio voices—the Easy Aces, pushing Anacin like a doctor's prescription, Jack Armstrong, Baby Snooks, Lorenzo Jones, the inventor, and his wife Belle (a faint strain of *Funiculi-Funicula* here), Stella Dallas, Captain Midnight, and Sam Spade —have set up an everlasting static in some inner ear. It's the only reception left them nowadays. I frankly doubt if you get them on a transistor set, even if they should be hovering about on some ghostly frequency. Too plastic and puny. They needed the mahogany comfort of the old stand-up console that used to occupy one end of the living room like Fort Ticonderoga. They fed on a repudiated substance called ether, and resided in a band on the old disk dials marked Standard Broadcast. (Other bands were labeled Weather, Police, Amateur, Ship, and even Aircraft Beacon.) And they are as vanished as the console's electrical innards, which made excellent forage, at one time, for beginning radio hams.

Sometimes you can catch a five-minute vestigial trace of them on *Monitor,* or actually "see" a few of them, like Jack Benny and the Lone Ranger, on TV, but their unique qualities—which were strictly for the listening ear—are gone. How, for instance, would you ever "zoom in" on Fibber McGee's closet? That avalanche of roller-skates, vacuum-cleaner parts, and bot-

tles of Johnson's Glo-Coat, then the epic pause, and finally the falling dinner-bell: it was pure sound, and it's a relief to find NBC's innocuous revival of *Fibber McGee and Molly* keeping at least that closet sacred— and off-camera. Or Jack Benny's Maxwell. It was an internal combustion that Mel Blanc brought out of his own gut and had nothing to do with the visible automotive world. Or that door Raymond opened on *Inner Sanctum.* It wasn't a door. It was a ghastly rasp that climbed up your spine. Or better yet, The Shadow. How could he ever be televised? His alter ego, Lamont Cranston, wealthy man about town, that's feasible— he'd make a good guest on *The Jack Paar Show*—but The Shadow himself? I see a blank screen, perhaps a little misty—The Shadow clouding men's minds right in their own living rooms—or a bleak melodrama, the main character permanently missing from the cast— or, even worse, a strange boxlike figure stumbling through the set, dressed from head to foot in an echo chamber, the source of that Blue Coal voice.

No, The Shadow was pure radio, a vague persona scripted for that Gothic half-hour chiller that collapsed with the anthracite coal market. The Shadow went out with the coal furnace (whose fiery innards somehow seemed the perfect lighting for him), and station WOR, to my mind, never recovered. No more sculptors bathing their marbles in human blood for realism, or demented Ariadniks strangling people in the cult of the spider, or scientific gangsters reduced to ash in their own fricassee rays. About 5:55 p.m. on Sunday, the show wound up with the cornered lunatic emptying his derringer in The Shadow's general direction, save for a last round which he walloped into his own brain, "cheating the hangman." The Shadow laughed his weird laugh of bloodcurdling integrity, and was never hit. As I remember, his only close shave was with a mobster who picked him up on an early TV set. The Shadow smashed that one to smithereens, but a couple of years later antennae sprang up everywhere. *"Who knows what evil lurks in the hearts of men?"*

They haunt me still, those Gothic chillers—*The Shadow, Inner Sanctum,* and Arch Oboler's *Lights*

*Reprinted with permission from the April, 1960, issue of *Esquire*.

*Out.* (Are there any who remember the dropped test tube that started eating an ever-widening hole in the earth that hasn't, by any logic, stopped yet?) *Suspense*—which still survives on CBS—had one in particular, concerning "Donovan's Brain," that all but cut me out of my Hallowe'en when it was repeated one year. Donovan was a man of superior intellect, though dead, whose brain Ronald Colman & Associates had perking in the laboratory. The brain made a rich burbling sound like a pan of lentils, an eerie *leitmotif*, and all but controlled the world—Colman powerless to resist its ebullient bidding—before a bolt of levin got it. (The Hand of God—like many large matters—was something that could be "done" on radio.) But I never was really at ease about Donovan's brain until I supposedly "saw" it. They couldn't resist making a movie out of the story, and the film followed its unerring course onto *The Late Late Show.* I'll admit to being older by that time, but I'm sure, even to the moppet, the *visible* brain of Donovan must have looked like something the cook forgot to wrap up and put in the freezer. TV curdled it before lightning ever struck.

They were the pulp classics of the air waves, these shows, and nothing like them will ever be done on television because they demanded the very thing TV has scotched: imagination. The listener produced half the show right in his own head, taking his lead from a range of voices, a musical bridge, and a few sound effects. The viewer doesn't have to produce anything. It's all right there in front of him on the "big" screen—see!—and only an old-time listener can tell him what a narrow, little everyday vista it is. Alfred Hitchcock can reproduce *human* criminal types (even the Martians turn up as bartenders and newspaper reporters on his show), but radio could rush you right into eternal Evil. It had open to it the land of Faery, Weir, Mars, the Dismal Swamp, the Dark Side of the Moon, literally anywhere imaginable. Not just police records and the minutes of psychiatric clinics. These were no actual case mysteries to support *I Love a Mystery.*

Of course, you had to pass a minimum-age requirement—with me, it was eleven—before you could get parental permission ("They'll just give you bad dreams") to listen to these shows. (This isn't strictly accurate because there was a lot of after-hours listening. With the volume on the bedroom Zenith turned down to barely audible, you kept one ear warm by the heated dial, the other out for footsteps on the stair well. It set up a high-pitched buzz in whichever you favored as your radio ear, and lasted until you fell asleep in the middle of some thriller one night and they caught you next morning with a hot tube.) But most of us worked up to them through the fifteen-minute serials that were jammed between the last afternoon soap opera and the six o'clock news. You could usually knock off six of these in a row if you weren't being rationed. They all centered around a superman—Superman, in fact, was among them—and began with a clarion call, something like hautboys and sennets in Shakespeare. Superman came in after being

mistaken briefly—with sound effects—for a bird and then a plane. A flyboy named Hop Harrigan *did* zoom in by aircraft after radioing the announcer ("Pilot to Navigator! Pilot to Navigator! This is Hop Harrigan . . . coming *in!*"). Don Winslow of the U.S. Navy was piped aboard the network with full protocol, and Captain Midnight began darkly with the clock striking the witching hour at, I believe, 5:30 (E.S.T.). A better device, however, was song, which combined both hero and sponsor. Tom Mix, cattle boss of all us Straight Shooters, rode up, singing, "When it's roundup time at Ralston. . . ." But Jack Armstrong, that All-American boy, used a full chorus in what amounted to a minor anthem. I think it can bear repeating:

*Wave the flag for Hudson High Boys*
*Show Them How We Stand*
*Ever Challenging We Champions*
*Known Throughout the Land!*
>     *( Ra Ra Boola Boola Boola Boola*
>         *Boola Boola Boola Boo Ra Ra Ra )*
*Have you tried Wheaties?*
*They're whole wheat with all of the bran*
*Won't you try Wheaties?*
*For wheat is the best food of man*
*They're crispy and crunchy the whole year through*
*Jack Armstrong never tires of them*
*And neither will you*
*So just buy Wheaties*
*The best breakfast food in the land!*

Jack Armstrong suffered a sharp eclipse as war came on—you might get hooted off the sand lot for listening to him—but by the test of memory, I'd say we identified with him far more closely than we realized. After all, Jack was on leave from Hudson High, and we were much more likely to go on to high school than into the Pacific or the Far West. Uncle Jim took good care of him, despite the horrendous adventures, and Billy and Betty were always at his side. There was a safety factor here, lacking in *Captain Midnight* or even *Little Orphan Annie.* They were always together, usually in some form of transport, cabin of seaplane, a dugout canoe, etc., and individual capture was the worst disaster. Billy—always a bit of a mental lightweight—got picked off regularly, though even Uncle Jim disappeared once in Africa. It combined suspense with actors' vacations. Jack's only drawback was a rambling plot line. Nothing ever finished cleanly. Tom Mix, on the other hand, offered a weekly adventure that resolved itself every Friday. One in particular sticks in my mind. On Monday Tom Mix territory was suddenly invaded by a giant, who went around flattening whole towns. Hardly a problem for a cowpuncher, but it was wartime by now, and Tom Mix put his mind to it. By Wednesday it was clear bullets would not destroy this monster, but on Thursday Tom happened to notice the giant sitting on top of a building and thought it strange that the building didn't collapse under all that avoirdupois. On Friday we knew. The giant was nothing but a puppet operated from Japanese aircraft, which dropped bombs to flatten towns. The Straight Shooters cut the strings on this effort to demoralize America, and the Nips went down in flames. All the serials were fighting the Japanese by this time—even the Westerns.

But by far the best Western was *The Lone Ranger,* the first night-time show I was allowed to listen to. It never pretended to be adult. It just demanded that you be able to pretend. (There was also Gene Autry, but he sang too much, and whenever he went *"Back in the Sad-dle Again!"* you felt like slipping him a wad of his sponsor's Spearmint with a burr in it.) The radio Lone Ranger was a very grave individual—humorless, in fact—who really spoke only to Tonto, and Tonto spoke only to his prairie gods. They came dangerously close to being a pair of snobs, and that was the secret of their radio success. The Lone Ranger was never really part of the Old West, like the lawmen, saddle-bums, and drifters mired in TV-cowboy history. The Old West was slightly *beneath* him. It was represented on the program by humble voices, homespun voices, worried voices, even whiskey voices that turned to his rich baritone in time of need. He responded effort-lessly, anonymously—the masked stranger—and just as they reached around to shake his hand, he was *"Hi-Ho Silver,"* away, and out of the studio.

Nobody ever knew who the hell he was. It was part of the mystique, which led my sister to describe him as "very handsome, despite his mask." He had a silver mine where he molded bullets, and a hidden past as a defrocked Texas Ranger, but that was all that was known of his estate and history. He was never re-searched. There was a lot of debate around the sand lot about his exact identity, but secretly we didn't care. All of us knew that Silver was a pair of coconut shells on a sound board (we could imitate by slap-ping our thighs in time), most of us had heard that the radio actor wore a mask in the studio, and many of us were doubtful that Tonto was a real Indian. But it didn't matter. We kept faith even when one Lone Ranger died in an automobile accident (for a week, he was off on a secret mission, and Tonto ran things), and they gave his spurs to the Bond Bread announcer.

It was a shock, but in the long run it didn't destroy him for us, because we needed only one constant: the *William Tell Overture.* For years, the *William Tell Overture* was the Lone Ranger, just as a short bridge out of *The Flight of the Bumble Bee* was the Green Hornet as well as his houseboy, Kato. The two pro-grams—originating over Detroit's WKYZ—sustained themselves on much the same *élan,* and with a few of the same voices. The Green Hornet had a souped-up, low-purring roadster that was as fabulous to automo-tive mechanics as Silver was to ordinary horseflesh. The Lone Ranger shot the guns out of bad hombres' hands. The Green Hornet put them to sleep with a green whiff of his nontoxic gas gun. Justice without carnage. Nobody, of course, remembers a single plot. But they weren't important even then. (We weren't

taking notes on how to break into the local drugstore.) All that mattered was the ritual of adventure, every Monday, Wednesday, and Friday—consult your local newspaper for time and station. From there you took it yourself, out into the back yard for your own story line.

We didn't have much store equipment for these back-yard roundups either—not by half what the kids today can haul out of the Five & Dime for their TV war games. We depended on the mails for our basic kit. The medium of exchange was box tops of various cereal denominations, and it was agony waiting for the Captain Midnight Badge or the Jack Armstrong Bomb Sight to arrive. They were always a big disappoint-ment, but we made brave with shoddy goods. I remem-ber the Jack Armstrong Bomb Sight was pretty effec-tive against the cutout paper Japanese Navy that came with it—if you leaned over a little. Another program offered a periscope ring that was designed for watch-ing people approach you from behind. If you squinted very hard, and asked the same person to approach you from behind at several different angles, eventually you got a brief glimpse of him—before the mirror tar-nished. The Captain Midnight Badge was also a de-coder—a wheel within a wheel—and the program often ended with an encoded message concerning tomor-row's installment. It was hell to be left out.

It was phony merchandise in a phony world, but we took Radioland for real and found in it a certain permanence that seems woefully lacking in TV pro-gramming. The favorite shows, corny as they might be, did not betray you—they could be depended upon to remain familiar, not to live riotously—and you did not desert them. Mr. First Nighter always had his seat on the aisle—"Curtain time! Curtain going up!"—and the recorded locomotive roared into *Grand Central Station* every Saturday afternoon. Mr. Keen was for-ever tracing Lost Persons, and Ellery Queen never failed of a fantastically contorted solution to the crime after the guest Armchair Detectives had made their own wild guesses. For years Cecil B. DeMille spoke with the softness of his product in introducing the weekly scenario on *Lux Radio Theater.* Irene, the Singing Lady, and the Let's-Pretenders carved up fairyland between them, and Uncle Don read us the funny papers every Sunday morning. In fact, some programs were phenomenons of continuity. *One Man's Family,* for instance, went on and on and on, as dura-ble as Father Barbour himself. It expanded (thirty minutes) and contracted (fifteen minutes), but never disappeared. When they finally did try to take it off the air, it had to be returned by popular demand. In those gentler times there were a lot of durable family groups. Lum and Abner, Vic and Sade (with an uncle who sat on the couch and did nothing but leaf through old Christmas cards), Myrt and Marge, the Goldbergs, and Ethel and Albert. The Aldriches spent many win-ters raising their son, Henry, when the problems of teen-agers were still funny, not homicidal. Henry Ald-rich never went on a rumble. The closest thing to a juvenile delinquent was Baby Snooks. But she was pretty fearsome. In fact, the whole menage—Fanny Brice as Baby Snooks, Hanley Stafford as Daddy, and the unheard baby brother, Robespierre—had a sadistic streak. Baby Snooks would execute some torture on Robespierre—boiling him in his bottle-sterilizer, maybe—and then Daddy would painfully worm the truth out of her. The sign-off was Baby Snooks' bawling at the top of Fanny Brice's lungs as Daddy walloped her from here to Tuesday. For all its vaunted courage over old-time radio, TV has yet to raise its hand to a child.

Matter of fact, there was a lot of mayhem on old-time radio. It was the original era of the private eye, and they were loitering around every station break, oiling their roscoes, waiting for work like everybody else. The present generation of TV gumshoes, done to a background of cool jazz and fine tailoring, is only a pale shadow of the first idea. The original private eyes on radio were down-and-outers, real social rebels, even a little leftist. They stood for independence, hatred of cant, distrust of the State, especially the police, and breaking a few yeggs to make an omelet. The best of them, Sam Spade, got "his"—appropriately enough—from the House Un-American Activities Committee *et al.* But while he lasted, Sam was a hard-boiled wonder. Producer William Spier went back to the master himself, Dashiell Hammett, and directly translated. The shows were loaded with "characters" —dwarfs, grandmothers, drunks, even Brigid O'Shaunessy from time to time—and plenty of hardware. Spier even took extra air time once to do the entire *Gutting of Coofegnall*—a famous Hammett story, in which several top gangs join forces and stage a guerrila attack, with grenades, machine-gun emplacements, fire points —just to rob a bank. It was some caper, and Effie's shorthand could barely keep up with Sam's dictation. Sam was played with rough dignity by Howard Duff, who spent two seasons on TV clowning Mr. Adams to his wife Ida Lupino's Eve. Just another TV buffoon husband. Period, end of report.

And certainly radio was much kinder to the comedians than TV. Listeners were stubbornly loyal to their comics—they were old friends, not just sponsored clowns—and a lot more patient, less greedy about their humor. There was nothing we loved better than a running gag, and the longer it ran, the nearer to collapse, the funnier it got. As far as I'm concerned, one of the unsolved mysteries of Our Time is whether the polar bear in Jack Benny's cellar really *did* eat the gas man. It didn't take much to make us laugh. The least little tag or sound effect could break us up. "Good-*night*, Mrs. Calabash, wherever you are" (Jimmy Durante), "That's a joke, son!" (Senator Claghorn of Allen's Alley), "Uga-Ugaboo-Ugaboo-Boo-Uga!" (fraternal greeting from Mel Blanc), "Duffy ain't here. . . . Oh, it's you, Duffy" (Archie answering the telephone in Duffy's Tavern), or Mortimer Snerd's reflective, even consultative ". . . Pretty stupid, huh?" Only a few of them ever frayed out, though I quickly gave up on

Lou Costello's "Hey, A-a-b-bot!" after a brief infatuation with their "Who's on first?" routine. Of course, for the big laughs, you waited. They depended on familiarity, almost equinoctial timing. Fred Allen and Jack Benny feuded for years before Benny found his one great impromptu riposte to an Allen insult. "If I had my writers here, you wouldn't talk to me like that again and get away with it!" And Benny's stinginess really paid off the night a thief jumped out at him and cried, "Your money or your life!" The ensuing dead air was one of the funniest moments in radio.

Most of the radio comedians throve on clichés, which kept them rolling along even when there wasn't a new gag available. The flies in Duffy's Tavern, Eddie Cantor's daughters, Benny's thirty-nine years plus violin, Durante's schnozzola, Bob Hope's foul mouth (the constant rumor was that he might get cut off the air at any moment for a chancy roulard), and Charlie McCarthy's fear of ax, gimlet, and saw. (Charlie, if anybody, proves old-time radio's geniality. Ventriloquism is essentially a visual stunt, but Charlie came across much better as a voice on radio than he ever has as a dummy on Bergen's knee.) But the best of them, the late Fred Allen, made a cliché of radio itself. Only Henry Morgan, the slayer of a hundred sponsors, rivaled Allen in the suicidal spoof that presaged the end of old-time radio.

Perhaps we were really ready for it, even before television. The dirty jokes about Tonto and the Lone Ranger were already in circulation, and Frank Sinatra had been replaced by Lawrence Tibbett on *The Lucky Strike Hit Parade.* Uncle Don had made his famous remark to the kiddies—"That ought to fix the little bastards for another night"—without realizing he was still on the air. Things were busting up. But it was Allen who found the laughs in the plight. Most of radio—studio audiences, daytime soap operas, Dorothy and Dick, etc.—disgusted him. He answered back with his Oriental detective, One Long Pan, and anybody who has ever heard his sketch of the morning-sunshine couple who wake up with a hang-over—the husband ends up beating the children, and shooting the sweet-tweetie canary across the burnt toast—knows how deeply he felt. Allen was a funnyman, but what he really produced was a caustic, down-beat semidocumentary on his own medium.

In fact, old-time radio really ended at the foot of Allen's Alley, that twisted little by-lane of the public mind. Every Sunday, Allen, the weary pollster, strolled down there and knocked on doors with his tiny question. All he got for answer was bombast and opinionation (Senator Claghorn), small wit (Titus Moody), and female dizziness (Portland Hoffa), all the virtues of the great mass audience. It was hilarious, but it was a cul-de-sac. We could hear a whisper of ourselves, and we couldn't get out. The spell was broken. Something else had to come after.

What came after was television, and when they tried abortively to put Allen's Alley on the TV screen, they ended up, significantly, with a bunch of puppets.

# Part One: THE BEGINNING

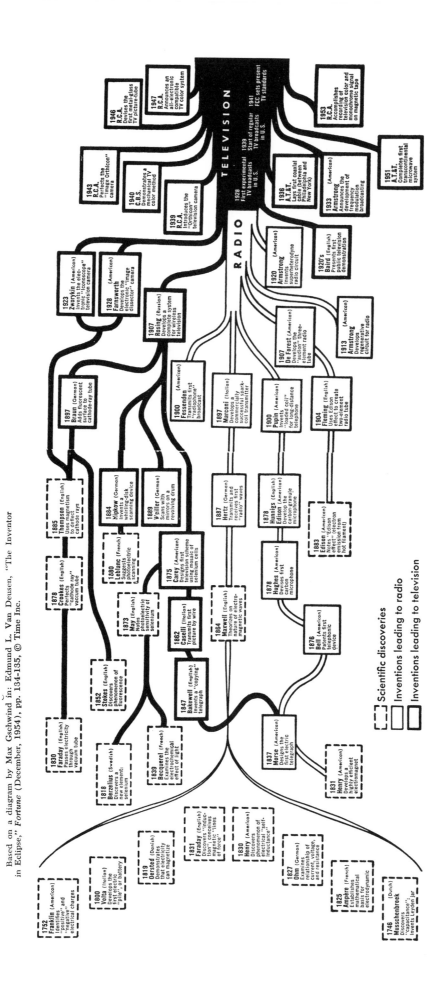

Based on a diagram by Max Gschwind in: Edmund L. Van Deusen, "The Inventor in Eclipse," *Fortune* (December, 1954), pp. 134-135, © Time Inc.

This flow chart shows why no one man can be credited with having "invented" radio or television.

- [dashed box] Scientific discoveries
- [white box] Inventions leading to radio
- [black box] Inventions leading to television

**TELEVISION**

1928 First experimental TV broadcasts in U.S.  1939 Start of regular TV broadcasts in U.S.  1941 FCC sets present TV standards

1946 R.C.A. Devises the first metal-glass TV picture-tube
1947 R.C.A. Announces an all-electronic compatible TV color system
1943 R.C.A. Perfects the "image Orthicon" camera
1940 C.B.S. Demonstrates TV color method
1939 R.C.A. Introduces the electronic "Orthicon" television camera
1953 R.C.A. Accomplishes recording of television color and monochrome signal on magnetic tape
1951 A.T.&T. Completes first transcontinental microwave system
1936 A.T.&T. Lays first coaxial cable between Philadelphia and New York
1933 (American) Armstrong Announces the development of frequency modulation broadcasting

**RADIO**

1920 (American) Armstrong Invents superheterodyne radio circuit
1920's Baird (English) Presents first public television demonstration
1923 Zworykin (American) Invents the electronic "Iconoscope" television camera
1928 Farnsworth (American) Develops the electronic "image dissector" camera
1907 Rosing (Russian) Develops complete system for wireless television
1907 De Forest (American) Develops the "audion" three-element radio tube
1913 Armstrong (American) Develops regenerative circuit for radio
1900 Fessenden (American) Transmits first "radiophone" broadcast
1897 Braun (German) Adds fluorescent surface to cathode-ray tube
1897 Marconi (Italian) Develops a commercially successful spark coil transmitter
1900 Pupin (American) Invents "loaded coil" for long-distance telephone
1904 Fleming (English) Uses Edison effect to create two-element radio tube
1884 Nipkow (German) Invents a whirling-disk scanning device
1889 Weiller (German) Scans mirrors on a revolving drum
1885 Thompson (English) Uses magnetism to deflect cathode rays
1878 Crookes (English) Perfects "cathode ray" vacuum tube
1887 Hertz (German) Transmits and receives first "radio" waves
1878 Hunnigs (English) Develops the carbon granule microphone
1883 Edison (American) Notes "Edison effect" electron emission from hot filament
1875 Carey (American) Designs first television scheme using mosaic of selenium cells
1880 Leblanc (French) Suggests photoelectric scanning
1873 May (English) Notes photoelectric sensitivity of selenium
1862 Caselli (Italian) Transmits first picture by wire
1864 Maxwell (English) Theorizes on nature of electro-magnetic waves
1878 Hughes (American) Devises first carbon microphone
1876 Bell (American) Patents first telephonic device
1852 Stokes (English) Discovers phenomenon of fluorescence
1847 Bakewell (English) Invents a "copying" telegraph
1830 Faraday (English) Passes electricity through vacuum tube
1818 Berzelius (Swedish) Discovers new element: selenium
1839 Becquerel (French) Examines the electrochemical effect of light
1837 Morse (American) Designs the first electric telegraph
1831 Henry (American) Develops a highly efficient electromagnet
1752 Franklin (American) Identifies "positive" and "negative" electrical charges
1800 Volta (Italian) Develops the first electric "pile", or battery
1819 Oersted (Danish) Demonstrates that electricity can magnetize
1831 Faraday (English) Discovers "induction"; conceives magnetic "lines of force"
1830 Henry (American) Discovers phenomenon of electrical "self-inductance"
1827 Ohm (German) Examines relationship of current, voltage, and resistance
1825 Ampère (French) Establishes mathematical basis for electrodynamic
1746 Musschenbroek (Dutch) Discovers "capacitance"; invents Leyden jar

# The Beginning

Among the multitudes of living creatures that inhabit the earth, man alone has developed the faculty of precise communication. Indeed, it is this very attribute which promoted and furthered his progress. His ability to impart his thoughts, his achievements, and his hostilities differentiated man from beast. This gave rise to primitive society and prompted man's eventual conquest of the elements.

Undoubtedly, military requirements—the need to transmit signals to distant troops with rapidity and accuracy—led to the introduction of communication devices. Ancient man used fire, smoke, and drums to transmit his signals. The Argonauts used colored sails on their ships to convey meanings. The Greeks, Romans, and Aztecs used relay runners. In the days of Julius Caesar sentinels were stationed on towers at regular intervals to shout messages from one to another, covering as much as one hundred and fifty miles in a few hours.

Later, and as recently as 500 B.C., man made cunning use of bells, flags, and drums. At that time, Sun Tzu, a contemporary of Confucius and considered one of the greatest of Chinese military experts, wrote, "The control of large numbers is like that of small numbers, if we subdivide them. If we use the drum, bell, and flag, it is possible to control large forces at a distance, the same as small forces. According to old books of war, the drum and bell are used as the voice, while flags are used to assist in seeing. The use of bells, drums, banners, and flags is to unite and attract the eye and ear."

During the time of Aristotle, the ancient Greeks developed an ingenious method of transmitting official signals between ships and shore and between ships at sea by the use of flags. This system was further developed by Polybius (in 200 B.C.), permitting the communication of precise messages, using the Greek alphabet. The method was limited, however, to comparatively short distances—that is, as far as the eye could see. Records also indicate the use of carrier pigeons for message-sending over much wider distances, frequently up to thousands of miles. Early methods of communications, however, were all slow, and man rebelled against the limitations of time and space, constantly seeking new methods.

In medieval times, knights flashed their burnished shields in the sunlight to communicate with each other. During the fourteenth century, considered to be the beginning era of gunpowder, the cannon was used to send audible signals. The firing of a predetermined number of guns was used to coordinate the activities of military forces. Frequently, when medieval towns were threatened with attack, the continuous ringing of bells was used. Trumpet and drum sounds, in use from the days of early civilization, played an important role in communications as recently as the Napoleonic wars.

Another method of signalling which was widely, used for centuries was the heliograph. This device flashed reflected sunlight in any direction over a distance of approximately seven miles. The American Indian signalled by day with puffs of smoke and by night with the waving of torches and with the shooting of flaming arrows into the sky.

However, the first really efficient system of transmitting messages was developed by Claude Chappe in 1794, and adopted by the French government. Chappe mounted semaphores on high towers, spacing them five miles apart. Each tower was equipped with cross arms similar to our modern railroad semaphores except that they were built on a much larger scale. These cross arms could be set so as to represent different letters of the alphabet and were read by means of telescopes. Messages were sent quickly and efficiently, limited only by weather and dark of night. Nicholas I of Russia liked the system so well that he built two hundred and twenty stations from the Austrian border through Warsaw to St. Petersburg.

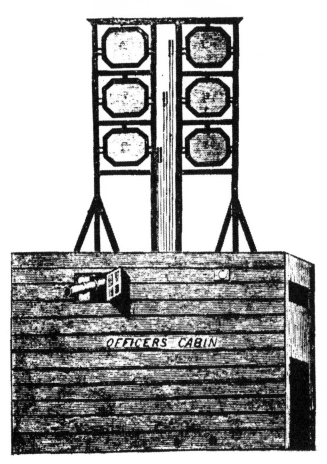

An early English semaphore-telegraph station.

## Signals Through the Air

In 1267, Roger Bacon, a scientist and writer, conceived of the possibility of using electricity for communications. He wrote extensively on the subject in one of his many popular books, and the idea was so revolutionary that he was imprisoned for dealing in black magic.

In the mid-sixteenth century, an era still rampant with superstition, Giovanni Battista Della Porta, a young man endowed with a compulsive sense of curiosity, wrote a book on "natural magic." He described a unique method of using *magnetism*, a phenomenon recognized since ancient times, to transmit messages. He termed it *sympathetic telegraph*. The idea was a curious one and aroused both skepticism and amusement among his contemporaries. Essentially, it was purely speculative and lacked more advanced scientific knowledge and the pressures of necessity.

The Burgomaster of Magdeburg, Germany, Otto von Guericke, produced an electricity-producing machine in 1672. He constructed a globe of sulphur that could be revolved by turning a crank. Rubbing his hands upon the sulphur ball as it revolved, he actually produced electricity in a manner similar to our modern

generators. Other investigators continued to study and to try new forms of friction machines. Anthony Wood of England discovered in 1726 that electricity could be conveyed by a metal conductor, and a few years later Stephen Gray and Charles Dufay sent electricity through eight hundred feet of wire, thus establishing the first basic principle of telegraphy.

The exact origin of the Leyden jar, which made storing electricity possible and which eventually evolved into the modern storage battery and power house, is unknown. Some historians say that the jar was invented by Dean von Kleist of the Cathedral of Kamin in 1745. However, others credit the invention to Professor Musschenbroek of Leyden. According to this version, Musschenbroek, while conducting an electrical experiment in January 1746, tried to inject an electrical charge into a glass bottle of water. His associate was holding the bottle in one hand when Musschenbroek by chance attached the charged conductor of the friction machine with the other hand. The result was that the man received a violent electric shock. This accidental discovery led to the development of the Leyden jar. Benjamin Franklin n 1752 demonstrated that a lightning flash from cloud to earth had a similar electrical charge to that contained in the Leyden jar. Franklin also mused over the possibility of using electricity as a means of communication.

The nineteenth century and its development of industrialization created the need for a speedy method of communication. The discovery of the electric magnet at that time made telegraphy a scientific possibility. During this period, literally hundreds of men carried the study of electricity forward, each adding something new. Oersted showed that current exerts a force which would deflect a magnet. La Place advanced the idea that a magnetic needle might be developed to receive messages at a great distance. Ampere put magnetic needles at the ends of twenty-six wires so that the needle deflections could signal the letters of the alphabet. In 1820 Baron Schilling, a

The electromagnet is the basis of modern telegraphy. This is the first electromagnetic telegraph system (1832).

Hussar captain, produced a telegraphic instrument which he operated with five magnetic needles.

In 1826 on Long Island, New York, Harrison Grey Dyar operated a telegraph line. A little later Joseph Henry, an Albany schoolmaster, developed the operation of an electromagnetic telegraph. He operated his instrument between two buildings at Princeton University in 1836. Gauss and Weber devised a simple magnetic telegraph in 1833 at the University of Goettingen. In 1836 Steinhul made numerous improvements on their instruments. The following year, Sir Charles Wheatstone and Sir William Cooke obtained a patent in England for their telegraph instrument, the first ever to be used in that country.

Thus the stage was set for an obscure American Professor of the Arts, Samuel F. B. Morse at New York University, to develop a practical electromagnetic telegraph system. In 1835 Morse proved that signals could be transmitted by wire. As in the case of many notable inventions, he had difficulty in arousing the scientific world. Driven by a fierce desire to gain the national acceptance of his invention, Morse gave a public demonstration, only to be ridiculed and re-

Samuel F. B. Morse, who invented the first practical electromagnetic telegraph system.

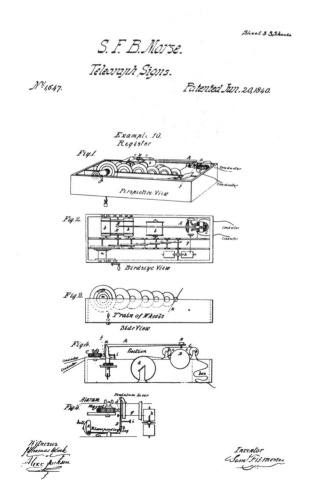

A sheet from Morse's patent form for the telegraph.

buffed by the world around him. It was not until five years later that Congress recognized the possibilities of telegraphy and appropriated thirty thousand dollars to construct an experimental telegraph line from Washington to Baltimore. "What hath God wrought?" was the first message Morse clicked out by electromagnetic telegraph.

The days of the pony express, carrier pigeon, and semaphore were numbered. The colorful pony express required ten and a half days to carry a message from St. Joseph, Missouri, to San Francisco. The stage coaches required forty-four hours to bring news from New York to Washington. The electromagentic telegraph transmitted signals almost instantaneously. At last the chains which slowed the development of communications to a snail's pace were broken, permitting the eventual invention and growth of radio and television.

Three days after Morse's historic message from the old Supreme Court Chamber in the United States Capitol, a dramatic incident occurred which demonstrated to the world the tremendous value of telegraphy. The Democratic national convention was held in Baltimore. Martin Van Buren seemed the likely choice, but James Polk won the nomination. When the

**Photo of Original Tape, now in Congressional Library, on which First Telegram was written by Samuel F. B. Morse**

In 1843 Samuel F. B. Morse, the inventor of the Magnetic Telegraph, received permission from the BALTIMORE & OHIO RAILROAD to lay, or string, four telegraph wires along its right-of-way, from Baltimore to Washington. The terminals were in the Pratt St. Depot of the Railroad in Baltimore, and in the Supreme Court Chamber of the Capitol, in Washington.

Morse had asked his friend, Annie G. Ellsworth, daughter of the Commissioner of Patents, to indite the First Message. It was

she who had first brought the word to Morse that Congress had voted him a grant of $30,000, so that he might demonstrate the practicability of his invention. Miss Ellsworth chose the phrase, "WHAT HATH GOD WROUGHT" (Book of Numbers 23:23, in the Bible) and it was this message that Morse sent in the old alphabet code, May 24, 1844.

Verification of this is given in his own hand writing, above, on this message that will live through the ages.

The original tape on which the first telegram was written by Samuel F. B. Morse.

news was telegraphed to Washington, skeptics refused to believe it. But hours later, people arriving by train from Baltimore confirmed the news, demonstrating the incredible speed of the telegraph. Raising money to establish a company was no longer a problem for Morse.

Morse and his associates extended their line to Philadelphia and New York. Later, small telegraph companies sprang up in the East, South and Midwest. Dispatching of trains by telegraph started in 1851, the same year that the corporate body now known as Western Union commenced operations. The year 1861 saw the building of the first transcontinental telegraph line, mainly along railroad tracks.

The telegraph provided speedy communication at a time when the West was becoming a new frontier. It aided in the extension and operation of the railroads. Side by side, the iron rail and iron wire pushed over plain and through the wilderness to make new settlements possible and to bring regions into closer contact. This unique and remarkable association of telegraph and railroad built up new communities, opened new markets, and aided in the vast expansion of commerce.

The original Morse telegraph printed code on tape. However, in the United States the operation developed into sending by key and receiving by ear. Until the advent of the telephone, which was intro-

As the telegraph wire stretched across the country the days of the Pony Express were numbered.

A replica of the instrument Morse used to send the first public telegraph message in 1844.

duced by Alexander Graham Bell in 1876, all rapid long distance communication depended upon the telegraph.

Samuel F. B. Morse, also pioneered in submarine

Music by electric telegraph was envisaged as early as 1850. The caption on this drawing remarked that "it appears that songs and pieces of music are now sent from Boston to New York by Electric Telegraph. Our American brethren have among them such remarkable musical instruments, and in fact such astounding lyres, that nothing can take us by surprise. . . .

"The great point of the invention, however, seems to be that if songs can be carried along the lines, our popular vocalists may treble or quintuple their present salaries by singing in four or five places at once."

The writer had his tongue in his cheek, but his facetious prophecy would come true not too many years later.

The stern of H.M.S. *Agamemnon*, showing the great drum from which the transatlantic cable was spun out.

telegraphy and demonstrated that an ocean cable could be a seagoing extension of the land telegraph system, to link islands and continents. With an insulated copper wire, Morse demonstrated that electrical impulses could be sent under water. Inspired by Morse's demonstration, private subscribers in New York and London raised capital, and an attempt was made in 1857 to lay a cable under the Atlantic Ocean. The cable broke after 335 miles of it had been laid by a ship operating from Ireland. Repeated attempts failed. Undaunted, Cyrus W. Field, leading the operation on July 27, 1866, succeeded in laying a cable from Ireland to Newfoundland. Returning to the mid-Atlantic, the ship located and raised the cable used in an earlier attempt, spliced it, and extended it to Newfoundland, thus linking America and Europe with two cables. Other transatlantic cables followed. Cable contact with the West Indies and Central and South America was established in 1882. The first and only transpacific cable connection from the United States was completed in 1906. Cable communication did for the linked continents what land telegraph accomplished domestically. International commerce was stimulated and the exchange of news became a matter of minutes instead of weeks.

Another view of the *Agamemnon* as she laid the Atlantic cable.

# The New-York

VOL. XV......NO. 4631. NEW-YORK, MONDAY, JULY 30,


## THE ATLANTIC CABLE.

### Successful Completion of the Great Work.

**The Old and New Worlds Joined Together.**

**Perfect Working Throughout The Line.**

**London Dispatches of Friday Received.**

**History of the Voyage Across the Ocean.**

**Wonderfully Fortunate Condition of the Weather.**

**Daily Record of Miles of Cable Laid.**

**Congratulatory Dispatches from Cyrus W. Field**

**Dispatch to President Johnson and His Reply.**

**Dispatch to Secretary Seward and His Reply.**

**The Old Cable to be Taken Up and Finished.**

**The Line Soon to be Open to the Public.**

[We announced in a postscript to the TIMES of yesterday morning the suspicious event here more particularly recorded—*the landing and successful working of the Atlantic Cable.* This news should have reached us on Friday afternoon, but there is a gap of 90 miles between Cape Breton and Newfoundland, where there is no telegraph cable, so that dispatches must be brought by steamer from Port au Basque to Aspy Bay. Below we give all that has been received, and as the news yacht returned last

11° 8'; distance from the telegraph house at Valentia, 27¾ miles; 29¾ miles of cable paid out.

WEDNESDAY, 11TH INST.—H. M. S. *Racoon*, arrived at Bearhaven to render all assistance in her power.

**Prayers for Success.**

THURSDAY, 12TH INST.—The *Great Eastern, Medway, Albany, Terrible* and *Racoon*, near one another. Services held at Valentia and prayers offered up for the successful laying of the cable.

**Connecting the Shore End with the Main Cable on the Great Eastern.**

FRIDAY, THE 13TH.—The shore end was connected to the main cable on board the *Great Eastern*, and at 2:40 P. M. the telegraph fleet started for New-Foundland, and the *Racoon* returned to Valentia.

**The Start—Order of Sailing—Condition of the Weather.**

The telegraph fleet sailed in the following order: The *Terrible* ahead of the *Great Eastern*, on the starboard bow, the *Medway* on the port, and the *Albany* on the starboard quarter. Weather thick and foggy, with heavy rains.

**Signals Perfect through 2,440 Miles of Cable.**

Signals sent through the cable on board the *Great Eastern*, and to the telegraph house at Valentia. Two thousand four hundred and forty nautical miles found perfect.

**Distance Run and Miles of Cable Laid Each Day.**

SATURDAY, 14TH.—Distance run, 108 miles; cable paid out, 116 miles.

SUNDAY, 15TH.—Distance run, 128 miles; cable paid out, 139 miles.

MONDAY, 16TH.—Distance run, 115 miles; cable paid out, 137 miles.

TUESDAY, 17TH.—Distance run, 118 miles; cable paid out, 138 miles.

WEDNESDAY, 18TH.—Distance run, 105 miles; cable paid out, 125 miles.

THURSDAY, 19TH.—Distance run, 122 miles; cable paid out, 129 miles.

FRIDAY, 20TH.—Distance run, 117 miles; cable paid out, 127 miles.

SATURDAY, 21ST.—Distance run, 122 miles; cable paid out, 136 miles.

SUNDAY, 22D.—Distance run, 123 miles; cable paid out, 133 miles.

MONDAY, 23D.—Distance run, 121 miles; cable paid out, 138 miles.

TUESDAY, 24TH.—Distance run, 121 miles; cable paid out, 135 miles.

WEDNESDAY, 25TH.—Distance run, 112 miles; cable paid out, 130 miles.

THURSDAY, 26TH.—Distance run, 128 miles; cable paid out, 134 miles.

FRIDAY, 27TH.—Distance run, 112 miles; cable paid out, 118 miles; which, with shore end off Valentia, distance 27 miles, cable paid out 29 miles, makes distance run 1,669 miles, and paid out, 1,864 miles.

**Arrival at Heart's Content—Average Speed During the Voyage.**

Arrived at Heart's Content at 8 A. M., Friday, July 27.

The average speed of the ship from the time the splice was made until we saw land was a little less than five nautical miles per hour, and the cable has been paid out at an average of five and one-half miles per hour.

The total slack was less than twelve per cent.

**Remarkably Favorable Weather.**

The weather has been more pleasant than I have ever known on the Atlantic at this season of the year.

We have had alternate days of rain, sunshine, fogs and squalls.

**Copies of the Diary for the Press.**

I have requested Mr. JOHN C. DEAN, Secretary of the Anglo-American Telegraph Company, to send

and Newfoundland, and hope within two weeks from this time to inform you that the cable lost last year has been recovered, and that a second line is in operation across the Atlantic. I assure you that all on board the telegraph fleet will do all that they can to accomplish this object. CYRUS W. FIELD.

HEART'S CONTENT, July 27.

*To the Directors of the New-York, Newfoundland and London Telegraph Company:*

We arrived this day. The cable has been laid across the Atlantic, and is in perfect working order. As soon as we have taken in coal we shall proceed to the spot where the cable was lost last year, and when recovered, splice it with the cable on board of the *Great Eastern*, and return to this place. Then the *Medway* will proceed to lay the cable across the Gulf of St. Lawrence. I cannot express to you how thankful I feel that you will now receive some return for the money that you have spent and the time that you have devoted during the last half year to connect by telegraph our own country with Great Britain,

CYRUS W. FIELD.

**List of Directors.**

The following is a list of the Directors of the New-York, Newfoundland and London Telegraph Company: PETER COOPER, CYRUS W. FIELD, MOSES TAYLOR, MARSHALL O. ROBERTS, WILSON G. HUNT. The officers of the Company are: PETER COOPER, President; CYRUS W. FIELD, Vice-President; MOSES TAYLOR, Treasurer; ROBERT W. LOWBER, Secretary.

**LATEST FROM ASPY BAY.**

**No More Dispatches from the Cable—The News Yacht Returns to the Newfoundland Shore—She will Bring Later Advices on Monday Morning.**

ASPY BAY, C. B., Sunday, July 29—8:30 P. M.

All dispatches from Europe via Heart's Content and Port au Basque, being merely relative to the successful laying of the cable, have been forwarded by telegraph from this point, and the News Yacht sailed this afternoon on her return to Port au Basque. Another vessel will arrive to-morrow (Monday) morning from Port au Basque with further advices from the cable and Europe. The telegraph lines are in good working order.

**PAST HISTORY.**

**Early Ocean Cable—First and Second Atlantic Cables—Failures and Lessons for Improvement—Differences in Construction—Beginning of the Present Voyage—What and Where is Heart's Content.**

The first successful submarine telegraph was laid between Dover and Calais, a distance of twenty-four miles, in 1850, since when a great have been built and successfully worked:

Of course, no one at that time dreamed of an Atlantic cable: that was further along—a younger brother, whose birth was as yet uncontemplated from the womb of time, whose prophecied coming even would have been received with shouts of "derisive laughter." In 1851 the columns of the London *Athenæum* contained a proposition from an adventurous speculator, who suggested that a wire, enveloped in a double coat of gutta percha and hemp, might easily be laid between the coast of Ireland and Newfoundland. The proposition met with no favor, but much discussion. The

SCIENTIFIC DIFFICULTIES.

in the way were such as to disarm the project of possible success. For instance: In the ordinary arrangement of the wires of the telegraph, where they are stretched upon posts, and insulated by glass and the surrounding air, the current runs along as a simple stream, and with a velocity almost inappreciable, while, when the wires are inclosed in a sheet of insulating substance, and placed in a metallic envelope or moist medium, the case is materially different. The influence of induction becomes a retarding power. As soon as the central wire becomes electrically excited, that excitement operates upon the adjoining layer of metal, or moisture, and calls up in it an electrical force of an opposite kind. Each of these forces

Prof. MORSE as electrician, and proceeded to connect St. Johns, N. F., with the lines already in operation in the British North American Provinces and the United States, by submerging thirteen miles of cable across the Straits of Northumberland, and eighty-five miles in the waters of the St. Lawrence. England and the Continent had already been connected with Ireland, irrespective of any design to extend the telegraphic communication toward the West, so that there then remained but a single gap to fill in—the Atlantic basin. The solution of the problem, where to cross and how to do it, thenceforth occupied the attention of the directors and the distinguished professionals retained in the service of the company. Without entering at all upon the discussions of many nice questions which came before them for determination—discussions which, in a scientific journal, would be both pertinent and interestingly instructive—we will state the results of the investigations. They taught

That gutta-percha covered submarine wires do not transmit as simple insulated conductors, but that they have to be charged as Leyden jars before they can transmit at all.

That, consequently, such wires transmit with a velocity that is in no way accordant to the movement of the electrical current, in an unembarrassed way, along simple conductors.

That magneto-electric currents travel more quickly along such wires than simple voltaic currents.

That magneto-electric currents travel more quickly when in high energy than when in low although voltaic currents of large intensity do not travel more quickly than similar currents of smaller intensity.

That the velocity of transmission of signals along insulated submerged wires can be enormously increased, from the rate indeed of one in two seconds to the rate of eight in a single second, by making each alternate signal with a current of different quality, positive following negative, and negative following positive.

That the diminution of the velocity of the transmission of the magneto-electric current in inductive-embarrassed coated wires, is not in the inverse ratio of the square of the distance traversed, but much more nearly in the ratio of simple arithmetic progression.

That several distinct waves of electricity may be traveling along different parts of a long wire simultaneously, and within certain limits, without interference.

That large-coated wires used beneath the waters or the earth are worse conductors than small ones, so far as velocity of transmission is concerned, and therefore are not so well suited as small ones for the purposes of submarine transmission of telegraphic signals; and

That by the use of comparatively small-coated wires and of electro-magnetic inductive coils for the exciting agent, telegraphic signals can be transmitted through 2,000 miles with a speed amply sufficient for all commercial and economic purposes.

With full faith in the power omnipotent of combined science and wealth, the celebrated Atlantic Telegraph Company was formed, mainly by the influence of Mr. CYRUS W. FIELD, who was sent by his American associates in 1856 to England with a view of effecting such arrangements as in his opinion promised best for the completion of the great enterprise. Three hundred and fifty shares of one thousand pounds each were taken, the charters, and grants, and privileges, and patents of the old companies were made over to the new, and everything that money could secure or science suggest was at its disposal.

THE ROUTE,

however, was yet to be selected. It's one thing to buy a horse and quite another thing to keep him; it's one matter to project a telegraph and buy the wire; it's quite another to lay the wire and run the machine. Several routes were proposed, but as they were rejected we need not allude to them. The one which gave the greatest satisfaction is known as the telegraphic plateau, which is only some 12,000 feet below the level of the sea, and extends in a continuous ledge from Cape Clear, in Ireland, to Cape Race, in Newfoundland; the greatest depth being in mid-ocean, whence it ascends imperceptibly to the shore on either side. To verify the information then in the possession of the scientific world, Lieut. BERRIMAN was twice dispatched in the *Arctic* to make soundings along the proposed line, while as a check upon his observations, Her Britannic Majesty's steamer *Cyclops* traversed the ground in an opposite direction. The knowledge thus obtained was conclusive. The plain was gently leveled, so deep as to be below the reach of disturbing superficial causes and composed of particles of shells,

On July 30, 1866, the *New York Times* reported the successful completion of the Atlantic cable.

Alexander Graham Bell, who became interested in telegraphy as a means of teaching deaf-mutes to talk.

Ocean cables were first operated by manually repeating the messages at points along the route. In
1921 "regenerators" were developed which permitted
direct transmission between terminals. Fewer than 300
letters a minute could be sent over the original transatlantic cable. Modern cables have a capacity of about
2400 letters a minute.

### The Telephone

Alexander Graham Bell, a handsome and intensely
serious young Scot, had emigrated to Canada and
thence to the United States. Bell lectured in Boston on
the articulation of speech by the deaf and gave in-
struction in his system. He was fired with the idea that
if deaf children could see speech they would quickly
learn to articulate. With this theory as a basis, he
developed the principle of the telephone with its
vibrating membrane. Deeply interested in telegraphy,
which permitted simultaneous transmission of code
over one wire, Bell was struck with the inspiration
that code was sound—sound which might be varied
in intensity of current, corresponding to the variations
in air density produced by the human voice.

Declared Bell, "If I can get a mechanism which will
make a current of electricity vary in intensity, as the
air varies in density when a sound is passing through
it, I can telegraph any sound of speech."

On June 2, 1875, after fashioning a makeshift dia-
phragm, he discovered that he could hear over a wire
the sound of a twanging clock spring. Nine months
later, on March 10, 1876, Bell transmitted the first
complete sentence. To his associate, Thomas A. Watson, who was in an adjoining room of their tiny Boston
laboratory, he said, "Mr. Watson, come here. I want
you." United States Patent No. 174,465 was issued to
Alexander Graham Bell on March 3, 1876.

Early efforts to popularize the telephone met with
failure. Although people paid to hear Bell lecture on
the "miracle discovery of the age," the country appeared at that time to remain unaware of its possibilities.

The year 1877, however, witnessed the erection of
the first telephone line from Boston to Somorville in
Massachusetts. At the end of 1880 there were 47,000
telephones in the entire United States. The following
year brought telephone service between Boston and
Providence. New York and Boston were connected
in 1884. Service between New York and Chicago
began in 1892, but not until 1915 was transcontinental
telephone service inaugurated.

Early telephones were leased in pairs. The sub-
scriber had to put up his own line to connect with
another listener. The first switchboard was set up in
Boston in 1877. New Haven saw the first regular telephone exchange in 1878. By the close of the nineteenth
century, the tangle of telephone wires in large cities
had become such an obstacle to fire fighting and the
wires were so subject to sleet and snow damage that
it became necessary to construct overhead cables. In
1888 it was possible to squeeze a hundred wires into
a large cable. Today, more than 4,000 strands can be
encompassed in a cable about the size of a man's
wrist.

Experiments with underground telephone cables
began in 1882, but it was not until 1902 that the first
long-distance underground cable was placed in operation—between New York and Newark, New Jersey.
The first cross-continent cable line was opened in
1942. There are now six coast-to-coast telephone wire
lines—two cable and four largely open wire. A number of deep-sea telephone cables connect this country
with Cuba.

Development of the telephone is strikingly revealed
in the evolution of its instruments. It is a far cry from
the streamlined dial handsets of today to the cumber-
some hand-rung wall models of a few generations ago.

It is an oddity that the dial telephone was invented

Camden, N. J. It appeared to the eye about three feet in diameter and passed from the south-east to the north-west. It was visible for about ten seconds, followed by a long trail similar to that of a comet. While passing it cast a light so great that persons on the street were led to suppose that there was a fire.

## AUDIBLE SPEECH BY TELEGRAPH.

### PROF. A. GRAHAM BELL'S DISCOVERY---SUCCESSFUL AND INTERESTING EXPERIMENTS BETWEEN BOSTON AND CAMBRIDGEPORT.

#### From the Boston Advertiser, Oct. 19.

The following account of an experiment made on the evening of Oct. 9 by Alexander Graham Bell and Thomas A. Watson is interesting, as being the record of the first conversation ever carried on by word of mouth over a telegraph wire. Telephones were placed at either end of a telegraph line owned by the Walworth Manufacturing Company, extending from their office in Boston to their factory in Cambridgeport, a distance of about two miles. The company's battery, consisting of nine Daniels cells, was removed from the circuit and another of ten carbon elements substituted. Articulate conversation then took place through the wire. The sounds, at first faint and indistinct, became suddenly quite loud and intelligible. Mr. Bell in Boston and Mr. Watson in Cambridge then took notes of what was said and heard, and the comparison of the two records is most interesting, as showing the accuracy of the electrical transmission:

**BOSTON RECORD.**

Mr. Bell---What do you think was the matter with the instruments?

Mr. Watson---There was nothing the matter with them.

B.---I think we were both speaking at the same time.

W.---Can you understand anything I say?

B.---Yes; I understand everything you say.

W.---The reason why you did not hear at first was because there was a relay in the circuit.

B.---You may be right, but I found the magnet of my telephone touching the membrane.

W.---I cut this relay out, and then the sounds came perfectly.

B.---I hear every syllable. Try something in an ordinary conversational voice.

W.---Shall I connect their battery in the circuit?

B.---No; there is no necessity to connect their battery in the circuit, for the sounds come out quite loudly.

W.---I am now talking in quite a low tone of voice.

B.---The sounds are quite as loud as before, and twice as distinct.

W.---Cut out the battery and then talk.

B.---All right. I will cut out the battery now if you will keep listening.

[Here an interruption occurred, and after a short time Mr. Bell said:]

B.---I thought you were going to say something.

W.---Is the battery cut out?

B.---No, but I will do it now.

[Battery having been cut out, Mr. Bell continued.]

B.---Do you hear anything now?

[Battery replaced.]

B.---Did you hear anything?

W.---No, not a sound.

B.---Say something to me when I cut out the battery again.

[Battery cut out.]

W.---....      ....      ....

**CAMBRIDGEPORT RECORD.**

Mr. Bell---What do you think is the matter with the instruments?

Mr. Watson---There is nothing the matter with them.

B.---I think...at the same time.

W.---Can you understand anything I say?

B.---Yes; I understand everything you say.

W.---The reason why it did not work at first was because there was a relay in the circuit.

B.---You may be right, but I find....that my.... touches the membrane.

W.---I cut the relay out, and then the sounds came out perfectly.

B.---I hear every syllable. Try something in a conversational voice.

W.---Shall I connect their battery in the circuit?

B.---No; there is no necessity for putting their battery in the circuit, as the sounds come out quite loudly.

W.---I am now talking in quite a low tone of voice.

B.---The sounds are quite as loud as before, and quite as distinct.

W.---Cut out the battery and then talk.

B.---All right. I will cut out the battery now if you will keep listening.

B.---I thought you were going to say something.

W.---Is the battery cut out?

B.---No, but I will do it now.

[Battery replaced.]

B.---Did you hear anything?

W.---No, not a sound.

B.---Say something to me when I cut out the battery again.

W.---I could not hear a sound when the battery was cut out.

[Battery replaced.]

B.---I fancy I heard a trace of your voice.

W.---Shall I put on our battery to see if it increases the effect?

B.---I'll tell you what we'll do. We'll take off our battery and put on theirs, as before.

[The company's battery having been placed in circuit faint and indistinct sounds were heard at the Boston end, and then came the intelligible sentence.]

W.---Is our battery off?

B.---Yes, our battery is off. What have you been doing? The sounds were quite soft at first, but now they are quite loud.

B.---Shall I put on our battery again?

W.---[Indistinctly heard.] That was very indistinct. Put on our battery.

[Original battery replaced.]

B.---We may congratulate ourselves upon a great success.

W.---Both batteries are on now. [Another sentence heard indistinctly.]

B.---Repeat the last sentence.

W.---Both batteries are on now.

B.---I understood that before, but I thought you said something else.

W.---Remove their battery, please.

B.---All right; our battery is the only one on now.

W.---I have put battery cells on here.

B.---How many cells have you there?

W.---S---i---x---six.

B.---Please whisper something to me.

W.---[Sound of the whisper clearly audible, but the utterance unintelligible.]

B.---I could hear you whispering, but could not understand what you said.

W.---Perhaps we have got the batteries opposed to one another. Had you not better reverse your battery and see what the matter is---or rather what the effect is?

B.---I will try the effect of reversing my battery.

B.---Is this any better?

W.---That sentence was accompanied by that curious crackling sound.

B.---Yes, I hear it too.

B.---What time is it by your watch?

W.---What are you doing? I have not heard anything except...for quite a while.

B.---I asked you what time it was by your watch. Perhaps you hear me better now, because I have reversed the battery again.

W.---My battery is now cut out.

B.---Don't you think we better go home now?

W.---Yes, but why does your talking come out so much fainter now?

[Mr. Bell here placed the magnet of the telephone nearer to the membrane.]

B.---Because I had moved the magnet further away from the membrane.

W.---That was very much more distinct.

B.---Will you try to understand a long sentence if I speak right on?

W.---I will.

B.---A few minutes ago I heard a fire-engine pass by the door. I don't know where the fire is, but the

B.---I fancied I heard a trace of your voice.

W.---Shall I put on their battery to see if it increases the effect?

B.---I'll tell you what we'll do. We'll take off our battery altogether and put on theirs, as before.

W.---Is our battery off?

B.---[Very indistinct---unintelligible.]

W.---That was very indistinct. Put on our battery.

B.---We may congratulate ourselves on our great success.

W.---We deserve success. Both batteries are on now.

B.---Repeat the last sentence.

W.---Both batteries are on now.

B.---I understood that before, but I thought you said something else.

W.---Reverse your battery, please.

B.---All right; our battery is the only one on now.

W.---I have six Daniells cells on here.

B.---How many cells have you on there?

W.---S---i---x---six.

B.---Please whisper something to me.

W.---I am now whispering.

B.---I could hear you whispering, but could not understand what you said.

W.---Perhaps we have got the batteries opposed to one another. Had you not better reverse yours; and see what the effect is?

B.---I will try the effect of reversing my battery.

[Battery reversed.]

B.---Is this any better?

W.---Much fainter, accompanied by that curious bubbling sound.

....      ....      ....

[Battery again reversed.]

W.---What are you doing? I haven't heard anything except that bubbling sound for quite a while.

B.---I asked you....      ....

....because I....      ....

W.---My battery is now cut out.

B.---Do you think we had better go home?

W.---Yes, but why does your talking come out so much fainter now?

B.---Because I moved the magnet further away from the membrane.

W.---That was very much more distinct.

B.---Will you try to understand a longer question if I speak right on?

W.---I will.

B.---A few minutes ago I heard a fire-engine go past the door. I don't know where the fire is, but the

number of the box is 196.

W.---The time by my watch is five minutes past ten. Had I not better go into Boston.

B.---Yes; I think it is time to stop now.

W.---Shall I go to Exeter place?

B.---Yes; but look in here on your way in case I have not gone.

W.---Let us talk conversationally without noting.

Conversation was then carried on for about half an hour with the utmost freedom, and the experiment closed.

number of the box is 196.

W.---The time by my watch is five minutes past ten. Had I better not go into Boston.

B.---Yes; I think it is time to stop now.

W.---Shall I go to Exeter place?

B.---Yes; but look in here on your way in case I have not gone.

W.---Let us talk conversationally without noting.

---

The October 21, 1876 issue of the *New York Times* reported the successful transmission of "audible speech by Telegraph," and reported the experiment made by Alexander Graham Bell and Thomas Watson. This was the first account of the use of a telephone.

Dr. Bell testing his telephone apparatus prior to a lecture in Boston. Cut-away shows his assistant in the basement.

1877

1878

1878

1879

1882

1887

1891

1891

1891

1895

1900

Representative Bell System instruments from 1877 to 1900.

by an undertaker—Almon B. Strowger of Kansas City. He devised it about 1889. The first dial exchange was installed at La Porte, Indiana, in 1892. Today about 77 per cent of domestic telephones are dial-operated.

Coaxial cable had its first experimental operation between New York and Philadelphia in 1936. Commercial service was inaugurated between Stevens Point, Wisconsin, and Minneapolis in 1941. It proved so successful that the American Telephone and Telegraph Company constructed a national coaxial cable network. The coaxial cable is designed to handle radio broadcast and television programs as well as telephone and telegraph traffic. One pair of coaxial units is presently capable of carrying 500 to 600 simultaneous telephone conversations or, alternatively, 9,000 to 21,000 separate telegraph messages.

Not many radio listeners are aware that few broadcast programs travel through the air exclusively. Most of them are sent over telephone wires, many across the continent. All types of broadcast stations depend upon telephone wire facilities to connect studios and transmitters.

In the early days of the telephone many cities and towns had rival telephone systems. Philadelphia was the last major area to give up dual service, doing so in 1943.

The first Bell telephone company started in 1878. It developed into the American Telephone and Telegraph Company, incorporated in 1885. The latter and its twenty principal telephone subsidiaries comprise the Bell System, which provides a variety of communication services.

In addition to the Bell System there are approximately 6,000 independent telephone companies and some 60,000 rural telephone lines and systems. The result is that the United States has more than 45,000,-000 telephones, most of which connect with the Bell System.

A song called "The Wondrous Telephone," published in 1877, humorously predicted the use of the telephone for transmitting music and lectures into the homes of America. Still to be realized is the prophecy in the lower right-hand corner—"Talking to the man in the moon."

### Radio Telegraph

Radio was a natural development of advances made in the field of electricity and magnetism. They paved the way for *wireless* communication, first by telegraph and later by telephone.

For many generations before Guglielmo Marconi, scientists knew that the leakage of electrical current in telegraph wires could "mysteriously" magnetize metallic objects at a considerable distance. As early as 1843, an American, Joseph Henry, succeeded in magnetizing needles with electrically charged wires located a distance of 220 feet away. Faraday in England performed similar experiments.

Widespread interest was aroused in the scientific world of 1865 when James Clark Maxwell, an English physicist, described the phenomena of electromagnetism, presenting evidence that electrical impulses travel through space in the form of waves. Maxwell indicated that the speed and form of the electromagnetic waves equal that of the velocity of light.

There were other pioneer experimentations and, in fact, a United States patent on a wireless system was issued as early as 1872. Thomas A. Edison took out a patent on a method of induction telegraphy in 1885. The inventor attached a tin-foil-covered plate to the top of a locomotive and with this device was able to attract "wireless messages" from the telegraph lines bordering the roadbeds. His purpose was to devise a means of telegraphing messages to moving trains. The Edison discovery was unsuccessful simply because the device attracted messages indiscriminately from all telegraph wires near the tracks, creating a jumbled collection of signals.

During the same period, an English inventor, Sir W. H. Preece, set up two squares of insulated wires a distance of 80 rods from each other. Through the wires he sent powerful electrical currents, causing an electrical signal to "jump" the gap from one square to another. It was, in fact, a crude form of wireless telegraphy.

A tremendous step forward was accomplished when

Heinrich Hertz experimented with electric waves and proved that they could be sent out at will around an oscillating current.

Guglielmo Marconi, developer of wireless telegraphy, at a receiving set in St. John's, Newfoundland. Here, on December 21, 1901, he received the first transatlantic wireless signal.

a brilliant German scientist, Heinrich Hertz, proved that electric waves could be sent out at will around an oscillating circuit. Hertz originated the theory of the existence of an all-permeating medium, which scientists call the "ether," through which waves of light and sound can travel. "Hertzian Waves" became the subject of numerous laboratory experiments that led some scientists to believe that telegraphy through space could be accomplished by employing these waves. Sir William Crookes predicted that receiving and sending instruments would be devised to make communication between remote points possible. This was in 1892, only three years before a brilliant Italian youth, Guglielmo Marconi, was able to overcome the many obstacles which lay in the path of practical wireless telegraphy.

### Guglielmo Marconi

Marconi, an intense young man privately educated in Italy and England, at an early age manifested a great interest in the science of electricity. He came from a wealthy Italian family and had both the leisure and the money for experimentation and equipment. In addition, his circle of acquaintances included many science enthusiasts.

In his teens, Marconi conceived the idea of the practice of wireless telegraphy. Even at that time, his life's ambition was to perfect and establish wireless communication throughout the world. His only fear was that other scientists might reach the goal before he did.

Young Marconi set up his first experimental stations in his father's garden. He built his own sending and receiving apparatus, and with this equipment he was able to transmit Morse Code via wireless waves for the first time in history. The Italian youth had discovered the great secret of wireless telegraphy.

Convinced that the discovery was more than just a laboratory toy, Marconi moved to England in 1896 and formed a company, after taking out a patent for his invention. Progress was rapid, and in 1899 he was sending messages across the English Channel. Two years later, he telegraphed the letter "S" from England to Newfoundland. This was the first successful transatlantic radio transmission. In 1901 he succeeded in sending signals across the Atlantic Ocean, and in the following year actual transatlantic messages were exchanged.

Marconi's success stimulated many others to develop rival systems, and patent offices throughout the world were rushed with applications for new wireless communication devices. However, Marconi alone succeeded in establishing a self-sufficient firm, and in 1899 the British Marconi Company established a branch in the United States. One of the major landmarks in the history of the Marconi Company was the acquisition in 1913 of its biggest rival—the De Forest company, which was called United Wireless. The company had succumbed to brankruptcy after losing a patent infringement suit to the Marconi Company. This merger gave American Marconi seventeen land stations and four hundred ship stations in America.

Marconi's activity aroused world interest. The result was that the first application of radio was established for marine telegraphy. In 1899 the United States Army established wireless communication with a lightship off Fire Island, New York. Two years later, the Navy adopted a wireless system of its own. Up until this time the Navy had been using homing pigeons and visual signals to send messages to shore. By 1900 a number of ocean steamships had installed wireless equipment. The first International Wireless Conference was held in 1903. The new medium of communication proved to be extremely effective in rescue work as well as in communication between ships and between ships and shore.

The first radio distress call from an American vessel was made in 1905. World news was made in 1909 when Jack Binns, a radio operator on the stricken steamship REPUBLIC, was able to summon aid successfully with his radio equipment. Later the same year, the S.S. *Arapahoe* brought help with an "SOS," using these letters for the first time as an international radiotelegraph distress call.

The United States Government was very much interested in Marconi's Wireless Telegraph Company of America, and after a demonstration, equipped all United States Navy vessels with Marconi equipment.

World War I brought about extensive developments. The popular imagination, particularly in America, was fired as never before. Mechanically minded individuals constructed amateur wireless sets, and these so-called "hams" proved to be important aids in the further development of radio.

Marconi had succeeded in freeing electric telegraphy from the fetters of wire and pole, and raised it to the freedom of the skies. No longer was it necessary for the Morse Code to follow a slender wire from sender to receiver. Instead, Marconi's inventions permitted the messages to be sent into the skies in all directions, to be picked up by any receiver which happened to be tuned to the same wave length. The next step was to discover the great secret of how to broadcast the human voice through the air waves.

*The Human Voice Through the Air*

Two Americans, Reginald A. Fessenden, a professor at the University of Pittsburgh and a former engineer in the Westinghouse Electric Plant in Pittsburgh, and Lee De Forest, a brilliant young Yale graduate, discovered methods which helped to achieve radio as we know it today. Fessenden had been experimenting with wireless, and in 1906 was engaged by the United States Weather Bureau to attempt to speed notice of weather conditions with radiotelegraph. He had already been of the opinion that the "coherer type" of receiver used at the time would be unsatisfactory for his work. The coherer was a glass tube filled with metal filings that had to be shaken down after the reception of a signal. Fessenden was working for a more effective substitute for the coherer; one which would produce electric energy with less trouble and with lower resistance.

He thought too that he might be able to devise a means by which the human voice and musical notes might be reproduced, a feat wireless transmitters then in use could not accomplish. He managed to develop a detector, which was actually a miniature electric light bulb having an exceedingly fine filament and possessed of the ability to reproduce voice undulations. While this detector was never put into commercial use, it did open the way to the invention of a subsequent detector and eventually to the transmission of voice and music.

It was Lee De Forest who invented the three-element electron tube, the Audion, which was to become the essential tool in modern radio. In 1883, Thomas A. Edison had discovered that a current could be transferred through the space between the filament and a metal plate sealed inside one of his electric lamps. He patented a device for measuring this current, but never made any further use of this discovery. Using Edison's invention, Dr. J. Ambrose Fleming, Marconi's brilliant technical adviser, devised a radio detector, the earliest version of the vacuum tube which eventually became the "soul" of modern radio.

De Forest began experimenting in 1903 with radio detectors and doing other engineering research work. By 1906 he had developed a three-element tube which could control the flow of electrons from filament to plate with great precision. His invention was a new type of wireless detector which was able to attain a range of four or five miles in sending voice messages. He had the good fortune of winning the approval of the United States Navy Department, which called him to Washington, and promoted the manufacture of several of his wireless sets for the Government. De Forest organized his American Wireless Telegraph Company with high hopes and great ambitions.

In the meantime, history was being made in the establishment of radiotelegraph service, which was

Dr. Lee De Forest invented the three-element electron tube in 1906 and named it the "audion." As a detection amplifier and oscillator (generator of radio waves) it made possible radio-telephony and broadcasting, and revolutionized the science of electric communications.

John Ambrose Fleming, one of Marconi's technical advisors, developed the earliest vacuum tube, which became the life and soul of radio.

inaugurated in 1901 between the five Hawaiian Islands. In 1903, a Marconi station was established in Massachusetts, and greetings were exchanged between President Theodore Roosevelt and King Edward VII of England. In 1905 the naval battle of Port Arthur in the Russo-Japanese War was reported by wireless, and in 1909 Robert E. Peary famous Polar explorer, radiotelegraphed to an excited world, "I have found the Pole."

Marconi opened regular American-European telegraph service in 1910, and two years later the first transpacific telegraph service was established, linking San Francisco with Hawaii.

The first telegraph service developed slowly, due primarily to the initial use of the "spark and arc" sets, which were unstable in operation, and caused much intereference with each other. The Alexanderson high frequency alternator and the De Forest tube were the answer to many of these earlier technical problems.

World War I found many countries experimenting with wireless or "radio," as it was beginning to be

# ew York Times.

RIDAY, OCTOBER 18, 1907.— EIGHTEEN PAGES — And Part L. of Autumn Review of Books. — ONE CENT — In Greater New York, Jersey City, and Newark, { Elsewhere, TWO CENTS.

**D BOYD**
**N STOCKS**

Brother Han-
of the Opera
Intendent.

**WIDE APART**

rhaps $300, Says
e'll Pay In
ne. **↑**

not getting rich
as Superintendent
Opera House and
any opportunities
lowing the antics
s in Wall Street,
sides having been
Opera House for
personal friend of
ded last January
ttle flyer in stocks
ay he is a sadder,
t the same fate as
ugh, he says, in a
ny of them.
theatrical business
made it a prac-
e for a rainy day.
e bank from time
o $1,000. Then he
nucleus made him
save, and another
vere added to the
ount had reached
rest bearing bonds.
when the stock
Boyd grew inter-
xander Conried, a
of Heinrich Con-
Metropolitan Opera

as no office, and,
as no direct con-
rage firm in " the
is known as a
king business from
d putting it where
is best advantage.
Mr. Conried $6,000
in stock specula-

onried bought for
mong the number,
y. The $6,000 in
$5,000, then $4,000,
000, and when the
ached, according to
m he would have
ney if he would
already put up.
ave Conried $4,000
al margins. This
had saved the day
ed the quotations
ch day he noticed,
stocks were get-
r. Finally he fig-
a large profit, and
r it. He says he
his point Mr. Con-
but adds that there
as Mr. Boyd had

de of the case to a
Vhen Mr. Conried
sented to give his
nd it is a very dif-
κes reporter.
Boyd were just the
other clients," he

---

# FIRST WIRELESS PRESS MESSAGE ACROSS THE ATLANTIC

### Signalizing the Opening of the Marconi Service to the Public, and Conveying a Message of Congratulation from Privy Councillor Baron Avebury, Formerly Sir John Lubbock.

Form 1C

## THE WESTERN UNION TELEGRAPH COMPANY.
INCORPORATED
### 24,000 OFFICES IN AMERICA. CABLE SERVICE TO ALL THE WORLD.

This Company TRANSMITS and DELIVERS messages only on conditions limiting its liability, which have been assented to by the sender of the following message. Errors can be guarded against only by repeating a message back to the sending station for comparison. and the Company will not hold itself liable for errors or delays in transmission or delivery of Unrepeated Messages, beyond the amount of tolls paid thereon, nor in any case where the claim is not presented in writing within sixty days after the message is filed with the Company for transmission.
This is an UNREPEATED MESSAGE, and is delivered by request of the sender, under the conditions named above.
ROBERT C. CLOWRY, President and General Manager.

**RECEIVED** at 343 Sixth Ave. Corner 46th St. •
TELEPHONE: 3907 BRYANT.

1B Lr Sn Dh & 53 Collect D, P R, Land lines,

London Via Marconi Wireless Glace Bay N S Oct 17th,

Times, New York.

This message marks opening transatlantic wireless handed
Marconi company for transmission Ireland Breton limited 50 words
only send one many messages received Times signalize event
quote trust introduction wireless more closely unite people states
Great Britian who seem form one Nation though under two Governments
and whose interests are really identical.

Avebury Marshall .............. 1210 Am Oct 17th

**ALWAYS OPEN. MONEY TRANSFERRED BY TELEGRAPH. CABLE OFFICE.**

The above message was immediately followed by others which appear in
another column of The Times this morning.

---

## MARCONI CONGRATULATES THE NEW YORK TIMES

**GLACE BAY, NOVA SCOTIA, Oct. 17.**—Mr. Marconi says: "Congratulate New York Times
on having received first westward press message."

---

## FROM THE PRIME MINISTER OF FRANCE.

**WEST STRAND, London, Oct. 17, via Marconi Wireless Telegraph to Glace Bay, N. S.**—THE NEW YORK
TIMES'S Paris correspondent forwards to me the following message for transmission across the Atlantic by Marconi wireless telegraph:

"Dans l'inauguration du prodigieux mode de communication mis désormais à leur disposition, les deux
grandes républiques ne peuvent que trouver une heureuse occasion de se féliciter et de formuler les vœux
les plus cordiaux pour le mantien de la paix dans le travail pour le bonheur des peuples dans la solidarité."
" CLEMENCEAU."

[Translation.]

In the inauguration of the marvelous means of communication put at their disposition from this time forward,
the two great Republics could not but find it a happy occasion to congratulate themselves and to express the
most cordial wishes for the maintenance of peace in the work for the happiness of the people in the joint responsibility.
CLEMENCEAU.

---

# WIRELESS JOINS TWO WORLDS

**Marconi Transatlantic Service
Opened with a Dispatch to
The New York Times.**

## MESSAGES FROM EMINENT MEN

**Prime Minister Clemenceau, the
Duke of Argyll, Lord Avebury
and Others Send Greetings.**

## 10,000 WORDS THE FIRST DAY

**Marconi in Personal Supervision
at Glace Bay and Greatly
Pleased with the Results.**

## SIR HIRAM MAXIM'S TRIBUTE

**His Message to Peter Cooper Hewitt
in New York, Who is Trying to
Pick Up the Oversea Messages.**

By Marconi Transatlantic Wireless Telegraph to The New York
Times.

LONDON, Oct. 17.—This message marks the opening of the
transatlantic wireless service. It
is handed to the Marconi Company
here for transmission to Ireland,
and thence to Cape Breton Nova
Scotia, and New York. As it is
limited to fifty word I can send
at present only one of the many
messages received for transmission
to The New York Times to signalize the event. This message,
from Privy Councillor Lord Avebury, formerly Sir John Lubbock,
follows:

" I trust that the introduction of
the wireless will more closely unite
the people of the United States and
Great Britain, who seem to form
one nation, though under two Governments, and whose interests are
really identical. AVEBURY."

**MARCONI'S CONGRATULATIONS.**

---

The first wireless press dispatch from Europe to the United States appeared in the *New York Times* on October 18, 1907.

The evolution of the De Forest audion tube to the Arnold
high vacuum tube.

called. Hundreds of radio transmitters were active in the United States, operated mainly by "hams." At the time they had nothing to do with entertainment, but were being used for experimental purposes and for transmission of messages for shipping companies and naval stations. For the Armed Forces, radio proved to be an excellent means of transmitting intelligence. As the war progressed, the value of radio was recognized, and a great post-war future was predicted. In most instances, people envisioned the medium primarily for sea rescues, for direction of planes, and for the exchange of messages over long distances. Few foresaw radio as an entertainment medium.

In 1912, a bright young wireless operator named David Sarnoff, received news of the *Titanic*'s collision with an iceberg. Sarnoff stayed at his key for 72 grueling hours and received the names of survivors from the rescue ship *Carpathia* as it approached New York. Four years later, in 1916, Sarnoff was working for the American Marconi Company in New York, and wrote the following memo to his superiors:

"I have in mind a plan of development which would make radio a household utility. The idea is to bring music into the home by wireless. The receiver can be designed in the form of a simple

Young David Sarnoff, in 1912 a wireless operator on Nantucket Island, Massachusetts, received the news of the *Titanic*'s collision with an iceberg.

'radio music box,' and arranged for several different wave lengths which should be changeable with the throwing of a single switch or the pressing of a single button. The same principle can be extended to numerous other fields, as for example, receiving lectures at home which would be perfectly audible. Also, events of national importance can be simultaneously announced and received. Baseball scores can be transmitted in the air. This proposition would be especially interesting to farmers and others living in outlying districts."

In 1916, these ideas of David Sarnoff seemed remote and visionary, and even in the year of 1919, when the Radio Corporation of America was founded, its main communication purpose was to send messages and not to provide entertainment or lectures.

The Radio Corporation of America acquired the assets of American Marconi, and was formed to give the United States preeminence and independence in world-wide communications. Its establishment was a national protective measure. Edward J. Nally became President of RCA and Owen D. Young, Chairman of its Board of Directors.

Many technical problems confronted the new organization. For example, amateur and commercial stations were creating virtual chaos of wireless interference. The United States Congress found it necessary to license sending stations, and to assign different wave frequencies for such stations. The ending of the war found this problem greatly increased. Ernst F. W. Alexanderson, the inventor of the alternator, declared that ether waves would "soon be as crowded as Fifth Avenue."

An amateur radio experimenter sent this letter on April 21, 1915, to the wireless telephone experimental station at Montauk, Long Island, New York.

President Woodrow Wilson, on the White House lawn, directs airplane maneuvers during a World War I demonstration of radio-telephony in 1918.

# Part Two: THE TWENTIES

The garage behind Dr. Frank Conrad's house became a test station for early radio equipment and programming. In addition to housing the station, the building provided a secret base for wartime experiments on U.S. Signal Corps equipment. After the war, Dr. Conrad broadcast his first musical programs from this garage.

In the four years before KDKA went on the air in 1920, Dr. Conrad, who was the assistant chief engineer of Westinghouse, used this transmitter to send out radio telephone programs. It powered station 8XK, one of the forerunners of modern radio.

Dr. Conrad at work in his laboratory a few years after KDKA went on the air.

# The Twenties

The decade following the first World War was a turbulent one for America and the world. In 1920 the Versailles Treaty went into effect, and the ill-fated League of Nations was inaugurated. War broke out between Russia and Poland, and Persia presented the first dispute to the League, demanding that Russia get out of Azerbaijan.

The Eighteenth Amendment to the Constitution became law in the United States in 1920, prohibiting the sale of intoxicating liquors. That same year women got the right to vote, in another amendment to the Constitution. In 1921 Nicola Sacco, a fish peddler and philosophical anarchist, and Bartolomeo Vanzetti, a shoe factory employee and radical agitator, were accused of killing two men in a payroll holdup at Braintree, Massachusetts, and one of the decade's most explosive trials began.

The early 1920's saw great developments in radio, and before the decade was out the new medium would have profound effects on the social and economic life of the country. The American people were just recovering from the many privations of World War I,

and the nation was entering an era of great expansion. Good times had come. There was work for everyone who desired it. The general prosperity of the country was the greatest impetus to the sale of radio sets and provided an excellent beginning for the new industry.

In 1920 the Westinghouse Electric and Manufacturing Company of Pittsburgh made its entry into the radio field. It established station KDKA, conceived and directed by Dr. Frank Conrad, Westinghouse's assistant chief engineer. Conrad, who had been a ham radio operator for many years, had established one experimental station, 8XK, in his garage in Wilkinsburg, Pennsylvania. During World War I, Conrad's station was used to test the military equipment built by Westinghouse. After the war, Conrad continued his wireless experiments. He made regular talks over the radio, and later began to play recorded music, to the delight of other hams. Then, to satisfy his listeners, he began to announce in advance a series of "broadcasts," —the first use of this term. When the broadcasts exhausted Conrad's supply of records, the Hamilton Music Store in Wilkinsburg offered him a continuous

# Air Concert "Picked Up" By Radio Here

Victrola music, played into the air over a wireless telephone, was "picked up" by listeners on the wireless receiving station which was recently installed here for patrons interested in wireless experiments. The concert was heard Thursday night about 10 o'clock, and continued 20 minutes. Two orchestra numbers, a soprano solo—which rang particularly high, and clear through the air—and a juvenile "talking piece" constituted the program.

The music was from a Victrola pulled up close to the transmitter of a wireless telephone in the home of Frank Conrad, Penn and Peebles avenues, Wilkinsburg. Mr. Conrad is a wireless enthusiast and "puts on" the wireless concerts periodically for the entertainment of the many people in this district who have wireless sets.

Amateur Wireless Sets, made by the maker of the Set which is in operation in our store, are on sale here $10.00 up.

—*West Basement*

This famous and foresighted advertisement, placed in the Pittsburgh *Sun* in 1920 by the Joseph Horne Company, stimulated public interest in Dr. Conrad's early broadcasts. The department store was interested in radio receivers as a new item of merchandise. H. P. Davis, a Westinghouse vice-president, was inspired by the ad, reasoning that the real money in radio lay in manufacturing home receivers and broadcasting programs to stimulate their sale.

supply of records if he would announce that the records had been purchased at the Hamilton store. Dr. Conrad agreed, and thus gave the world its first radio advertiser. By the late summer of 1920, interest in these broadcasts had become so general that the Joseph Horne Company, a Pittsburgh Department Store, ran this ad in the *Sun*, on Wednesday evening, September 29th:

### AIR CONCERT PICKED UP BY RADIO HERE

"Victrola" phonograph music, played into the air over a wireless telephone, was picked up by listeners on the wireless receiving station which was recently installed here for patrons interested in wireless experiments. The concert was heard Thursday night about 10 o'clock and continued about 20 minutes. Two orchestra numbers, a soprano solo—which rang particularly high and clear through the air—and a juvenile "talking piece" constituted the program.

This music was from a Victrola pulled close to the transmitter of a wireless telephone in the home of Frank Conrad, Penn and Peebles Avenues, Wilkinsburg. Dr. Conrad is a wireless enthusiast and puts on the wireless concerts periodically for the entertainment of the many people in this district who have wireless sets. Amateur Wireless Sets, made by the maker of the set which is in operation in our store, are on sale here $10.00 and up.

To H. P. Davis, Westinghouse Vice President who had been an ardent follower of Dr. Conrad's ventures, the ad was an inspiration. According to Donald G. Little, a pioneer amateur operator as well as an able Westinghouse engineer in the radio field, in an article in *American Heritage*, August, 1955, Mr. Davis reasoned:

"If this broadcasting [by Conrad] was of sufficient interest to the community for a well-known store to advertise receiving sets, maybe there was *something to it*. From there, Mr. Davis decided to build a more powerful transmitting station than the one used by Dr. Conrad at home, and try it out a little more thoroughly just to see what there was to this business—the thought being to promote the sale of home receivers."

### KDKA Makes History

Convinced that here as a great new business opportunity, Mr. Davis set about winning other Westinghouse officials to the same view. So persuasive were his arguments that a station was authorized, license application submitted October 16, and election night —then only a little more than two weeks away—was selected for the grand opening. KDKA went on the air with the world's first regularly scheduled broadcast—the Harding-Cox election returns on November 2, 1920. Here is a Westinghouse story describing the event:

The returns were received by telephone from a Pittsburgh newspaper, and were then sent out by wireless telephone. So rapid was the service obtained by this method that the receiving operators were able to get the returns exceedingly fast. In some cases they were heard even before they were received by special telegraph wires. During the intervals between returns phonograph music was played and those amateurs having loud sounding horns or two-stage amplifiers were able to throw the music over large rooms. Also two banjo artists were present and rendered very good banjo selections.

Not only in Pittsburgh were the returns heard, but in many towns in Ohio, Pennsylvania and West Virginia the

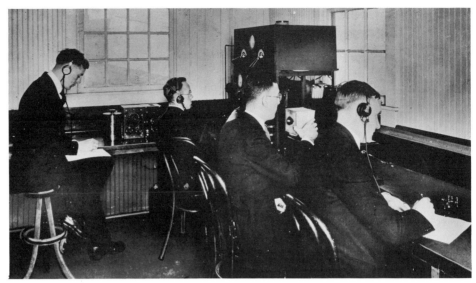

KDKA's broadcasting history began on November 2, 1920. This picture shows the station's entire staff and equipment set to broadcast the Harding-Cox elections.

messages were heard with equal clearness. Letters are still being received from operators from many miles around thanking us for giving the returns so promptly.

In Vandergrift, Pennsylvania, slide bulletins were shown in the street for the benefit of hundreds of people there, the news being shown from ten minutes to a half hour before they were received by means of an auxiliary telegraph wire between Vandergrift and Pittsburgh. In addition, the wireless set was connected by means of a cable with the local telephone exchange, and the wire chief sent the news directly to subscribers who had arranged beforehand for the service, and also gave the results to anyone making inquiries.

At Latrobe the message were utilized in a similar manner, thus enabling large crowds to get the messages early.

At Irwin a large hall was filled to its capacity to hear the results of the election, motion pictures being shown throughout the entire evening.

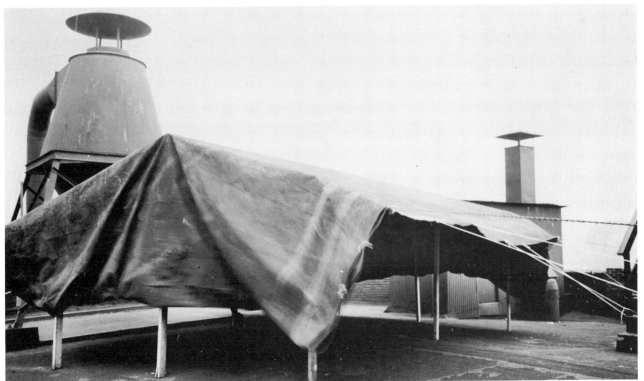

For the first six months of its existence KDKA was a radio station without a studio. Programs originated either as phonograph records or as "remote" pick-ups. As the demand for live entertainment grew, however, this studio tent was pitched atop the roof at a Westinghouse East Pittsburgh plant.

An experimental antenna carried aloft by a balloon was tried by KDKA at Saxonburg, Pennsylvania. The balloon later pulled away from the antenna, floated up and was destroyed.

Not only in the immediate vicinity of Pittsburgh were the returns as sent from the Westinghouse Plant heard, but throughout Ohio and West Virginia they were heard with equal clearness.

Also in Pittsburgh the radio method of sending returns was utilized in two ways. Persons having simple sets did not need to leave their homes to receive the returns, and by means of sets installed in a number of clubs throughout the city, large assemblages were able to have social functions while receiving the returns. At the Edgewood Club in particular a loud sounding horn was in use, and people could hear all over the large ballroom the voice of the speaker at East Pittsburgh as transmitted through the radio apparatus.

At the same time the wireless telephone was giving this news to radio operators, hundreds of men and women were receiving up-to-the-minute election returns in the auditorium of the cafeteria. As early as 8:30 in the evening announcements were made from several states as to how the election was going. The plan used to inform the people was very unique and thorough. As the returns were received they were thrown on the screen from the motion picture booth.

It was possible to receive the very latest returns through the cooperation of the wireless telephone service.

When returns were not being announced, a splendid entertainment program was in progress, consisting of music by Gill's Orchestra, motion pictures at intervals, vocal solo by Miss Ada France, vocal duet by Misses Ada and Agnes France and vocal solos by Miss Laura Atkin, Miss Anna Chilcote, George E. Kellogg and Fred Ward. Miss Julia Bartletti, pianist for the Community Chorus, accompanied the singers. The master of ceremonies for the occasion was A. S. Duncan.

Radio had demonstrated its potential impressively in broadcasting the election returns, and again in broadcasting Harding's inauguration ceremonies. Harding himself was intrigued with the medium and appeared frequently before the microphone. Fresh impetus was given to the industry's growth when the President delivered a series of important messages to the American public over the radio. Here was a tremendously powerful new medium for a political leader, permitting his voice to come into the very homes of the people. It was to affect the American way of life as no other influence had ever done before.

As an example of the potency of the new medium, the popularity of sporting events boomed as a result of radio broadcasts, which made it possible for an ever-increasing audience to remain in their own homes or gather in the streets hundreds of miles away and share in the thrills of a game. On July 2, 1921, the Dempsey-Carpentier fight was broadcast from Boyle's Thirty Acres in Jersey City through a temporary transmitter installed at Hoboken. Thousands of receiving

The first broadcast of WJZ took place on October 1, 1921. A room in the Westinghouse factory in Newark served as a studio for the program. Thomas H. Cowan, the station's first announcer and program supervisor, is seated at the piano in the same studio at a slightly later date. At the table is Joe Watts, Westinghouse engineer and announcer. Cowan, a radio veteran, is still to be heard on the New York municipal station, WNYC.

sets were bought just for this event. The announcer, J. Andrew White, gave the first blow-by-blow radio description of a boxing match. The Jess Willard-Luis Firpo fight in 1923 set a pattern for radio broadcasting that was to grow tremendously in popularity. Attendance at sports events increased greatly, too, their popularity stimulated by radio.

The number of stations listeners could tune in on grew rapidly. The Detroit *News* station, WWJ, which had been operating a radiophone, was granted a license for regular broadcasting in 1921. WJZ, then at Newark, New Jersey, broadcast its first program in 1921 from a small building erected on a factory roof. Its studio resembled a storage room, draped with odds and ends, old rugs, nondescript chairs and tables, and a rented piano and phonograph.

In 1921, KDKA, Pittsburgh, still located at the company's East Pittsburgh plant, did a series of "firsts" that included the first remote church broadcast, first broadcast by a national figure (Herbert Hoover), the

first regular broadcast of baseball scores, the first market reports, and the first World Series broadcast. Westinghouse that year produced the first popular-priced home radio receiver (approximately $60, not including headsets or loud speakers) and established radio stations in cities where it had manufacturing plants. These were KBZ, East Springfield, Mass.; KYW, Chicago; and WJZ, Newark. Incidentally, one station —now WBZ—remains in the original studio site at the East Springfield Plant.

The sale of radio sets grew so quickly that the manufacturers could not meet the demand.

In this period radio stations were not selling time for advertising, but were broadcasting primarily to stimulate the sale of sets.

Although the program which announced the election of Harding on KDKA in 1920 is usually considered the historic beginning of broadcasting, there are numerous other claims to this honor. Station KQW in San Jose, California, produced its first broadcast in

**Early broadcasting equipment.**

1909, and ran a regular schedule in 1912. Station 2ZK in New Rochelle, New York, was broadcasting music regularly in 1916. An amateur station 8MK, later to be called WWK, in Detroit, was broadcasting regularly more than two months before the Harding broadcast. In addition, both De Forest and Fessenden were doing experimental broadcasting before KDKA was in operation. However, KDKA was the first commercially-licensed station listed in the Department of Commerce records.

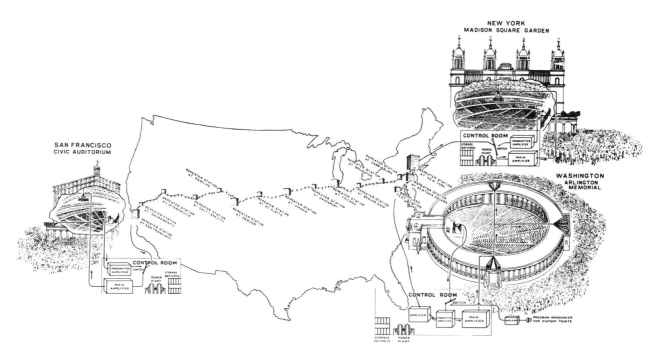

President Harding's Armistice Day address in 1921 was broadcast from Arlington Memorial in Washington to crowds in New York and San Francisco. This diagram shows the route of the telephone circuits used to carry the message. This was one of the earliest applications of the "network" idea.

Other organizations soon entered the broadcasting field; General Electric, AT&T, and of course, RCA, were soon in the broadcasting operation.

By the end of 1920, thirty broadcasting licenses had been issued by the Federal Government. Two years later, over 200 licenses had been issued, and in 1923 there were nearly 600 licenses. The main problem at the time was financial. No one had yet determined an adequate and regular method by which stations could support themselves.

During this entire period, the American Telephone and Telegraph Company had been watching broadcasting activities with a great deal of interest. The development of the radio and radiotelephony had been progressing steadily throughout the years. In 1922, AT&T financed and built station WEAF in New York, replacing another AT&T station, WBAY, which had proved unsuccessful because of its location. A great deal of money was put into the new WEAF, and many technical innovations were installed. It was at WEAF that many techniques of broadcasting and commercial sponsoring were developed. The company, anxious to test the potentialities of radio, inaugurated the policy of continuous broadcasting and sold time at the rate of ten minutes for $100.00. In one of the first sponsored programs ever to be broadcast, on August 28, 1922, at 5:15 to 5:30 P.M., H. M. Blackwell discussed the advantages of apartments in Jackson Heights, New York. In November of 1922, the New York Philharmonic Society broadcast its first complete concert, and President Calvin Coolidge gave his opening message to Congress, which was broadcast over six stations. On December 6, 1923, stations WEAF (New York), WCAP (Washington, D. C.), and WJAR (Providence, R. I.) were connected by wire, to become the nation's first network.

The era of expansion for radio had begun, creating one of the most extraordinary new product demands in the history of the United States. From all over the country, orders for radio receiving sets and for radio broadcasting equipment poured into the offices of manufacturers.

Said *Radio Broadcast* in its first issue, May, 1922:

The rate of increase in the number of people who spend at least a part of their evening in listening in is almost incomprehensible. To those who have recently tried to purchase receiving equipment some idea of this increase has undoubtedly occurred as they stood perhaps in the fourth or fifth row at the radio counter waiting their turn only to be told when they finally reached the counter, that they might place an order and it would be filled when possible. The manufacture is probably not even yet at its height. It is still growing in some kind of geometrical progression. It seems quite likely that before the movement has reached its height, before the market for receiving apparatus be-

comes approximately saturated, there will be at least five million receiving sets in this country.

Church services were first broadcast in New York City from station WJZ in January of 1922. During the chapel service in the Christ Episcopal Church, Glenridge, New Jersey, Rev. George P. Dougherty delivered his Christmas Eve message to the radio public.

In his autobiography, Vincent Lopez gives a colorful account of his first experiences with broadcasting. The year was 1921, and Lopez had agreed to help out his friend Thomas Cowan, who was then program director of station WJZ, by substituting with his band for a program that had been cancelled at the last minute. They wouldn't be paid, of course, but Cowan said, "There'll come a day soon when we'll both get paid—plenty. Wait and see."

A big payoff hardly seemed around the corner when we saw the WJZ studio that next evening. It was located in an old clock room in an unused area of Westinghouse's Newark factory. There were no elevators. Just a rickety stairway barely large enough for us to thread our instruments upstairs.

The small room was decorated with some absorbent material dyed an ugly shade of red to give it some semblance of uniformity. There were also some secondhand lamps as well as some rugs to help deaden studio sounds. Somehow an old upright piano had been squeezed in. Even Casey's in Brooklyn had owned a better one. But we were there, and we made the best of it.

 *    *    *

We had been so worried about everything else, we hadn't given a thought as to what the program would be. I'll never forget Tommy Cowan turning to me and saying, "Vincent, why don't you announce the program?"

"Me announce the program?" I was so frightened as it was, I didn't know what to do. Tommy and I argued the point for a few minutes. I told him it was my first time near a mike, but he finally talked me into saying hello to the radio audience. When the program began I stepped up on a little platform and said, "Hello, everybody. Lopez speaking." Cowan jumped up alongside me and said right into the microphone:

"Is that all you're going to say, Mr. Lopez?"

"That's enough for me," I answered.

Tommy took over as announcer and said, "The first selection will be 'Anitra's Dance' in a fox-trot tempo." I called out to the orchestra, "Number 42, boys," and we were on our way.

There's one other thing about that first radio show I'll never forget. Sometime during the program Cowan suggested that I play a piano solo. I motioned to the broken down upright and said, "On that?" But Tommy paid no attention to me and brought the mike near the piano. Well, there was no backing out then, so I played "Canadian

"Lopez speaking . . ." Vincent Lopez's radio career goes back to 1921, when he and his band played regularly over WJZ from the Pennsylvania Grill in New York.

Capers," the song which had been responsible for getting me the job at the Pennsylvania Hotel.

In those days there wasn't any specific time limit on programs. If something was good, it went on and on. Our show lasted an hour and a half.

◦  ◦  ◦

When the show was over the telephone started to ring. Many of the calls were from Westinghouse officials who were pleased with the show. I was still answering the congratulatory phone calls that lit up WJZ's undersized plug board long past midnight!

One call came all the way from Washington, D.C. It was from Joseph Tumulty, the secretary to President Wilson. Radio had no more ardent fan than Mr. Tumulty. He even came to New York a few weeks later to watch us broadcast.

There was some additional talent on the show that night —a young baritone doubling in radio to help advertise his appearance at a Newark theatre. His name? John Charles Thomas.

Tommy Cowan had quite an inspiration that evening. With the regular programs finished, he introduced Mr.

Tumulty on the air and interviewed him about the world political situation. Cowan chalked up another first for WJZ: the radio commentator.

Most of my band regarded our trip to Newark that night as a lark—or an annoyance. Paul Whiteman had already turned down such appearances for his band with the quick comment that radio was for kids, who liked to build crystal sets and fool around with them. I had a hopeful idea that radio would somehow increase our popularity, but I didn't foresee the millions of fans it would create for us within a few short years.

◦  ◦  ◦

The mail response to our music had the Newark Post Office working overtime for several days and Cowan asked us to broadcast regularly. However, E. M. Statler had no enthusiasm for that idea. He wanted us at the Pennsylvania Grill, quite naturally, not out in Newark.

"Can't you put a microphone right on our bandstand and send it out over the wires to Newark?" I asked Tommy, trying to hold on to the broadcast time.

"The telephone company says it isn't feasible," Cowan explained. "I think they're wrong about it. Let me see if Western Union can rig something up."

The rigging took a month and involved special wires out to Newark, but everything straightened out and we went on the air one Thursday night, with the announcement we'd be broadcasting regularly right from the Grill —another first—and we all wondered if people would like to come in and watch the band do a program.

Within an hour, telephone calls had soaked up every table reservation for the following evening—and the calls kept coming in that night and the next day.

Early Friday evening, Seventh Avenue and the two side streets looked like Ebbett's Field back in the old days when the New York Giants were fighting the Brooklyn Dodgers for the pennant. What's more, the entire hotel was sold out by mid-afternoon.

"Vincent," said an amazed E. M. Statler, "I couldn't build business up like this in a thousand years of hard work. You did it in an hour. I think radio has some real possibilities." It was the understatement of the century.

The first stage show for broadcast emanated from station WJZ on February 19, 1922, and featured Ed Wynn in *The Perfect Fool*. The comedian's reaction to the microphone was the subject of an article in *Radio Broadcast*, which said:

Ed Wynn approached the microphone gingerly. He looked at it suspiciously. The time came for him to perform. As with all professionals, he was a trifle nervous. The nervousness, however, wore off, but Wynn was appalled by the silence. He had told some of his best stories and had not even heard a snicker. He asked the announcer to help him and the announcer quickly assembled all the people from around the studio including the electricians in shirt sleeves, scrub-women, with their skirts tucked up,

One of the earliest programs on WJZ in 1922 featured Ed Wynn in *The Perfect Fool*. Wynn, born in 1886, has been in show business virtually all his life, starting in vaudeville and graduating into musical comedies on the New York stage. He starred in the *Ziegfeld Follies of 1914* and in many other Broadway hits after that. Wynn's type of humor, which he brought virtually intact to radio, relied heavily on outrageous puns and a giggling delivery. His trade mark, a long, drawn out "so-o-o-o-o," was interpolated in the telling of his fantastic yarns. In his Texaco "Fire Chief" shows of the early 1930's long-suffering Graham McNamee was his announcer and straight man. After many years of semi-retirement Ed Wynn has recently made a very successful comeback as a character actor in television and motion pictures.

Some vintage Wynn humor:

"A married woman? My goodness, everyone knows what a married woman is! That's someone who has nothing to wear, and six closets to keep it in. The wife likes clothes so much that one day when the husband comes home, she says, 'How do you like this new skunk coat I bought? It's genuine skunk. I bought it for a song.' He says, 'What's the song—"I walk alone"?'

"Here the mood changes, and the finish of the story takes place ten years later. They have an eight-year-old boy. He is always fighting with other boys. If he isn't fighting on one side of the street, he is fighting on the other, and he always gets beaten up. His mother almost goes crazy because she never knows which side her brat is battered on."

telephone operators and artists who were billed later on the program. They were all invited into the studio to view the show. It was a strange audience, but their approbation turned the trick. With the giggles, guffaws and shouts of merriment to encourage him, Wynn proceeded with the entertainment. He needed only the responsive sight of his hearers doubled over with laughter. Had he been a more frequent radio performer, he would have been able to imagine the fans in their homes tuned in on his program and convulsed with mirth.

Paul Whiteman entered radio about 1922 and his first experience in the WJZ studio also was somewhat disconcerting. The importance of the audience in the

Paul Whiteman, called "The King of Jazz," entered radio about 1922, doing his first broadcast from WJZ. In the next quarter of a century there was hardly a year he couldn't be heard on the radio and he became one of the pioneers in the new medium of television. Here he is before a broadcast in the 1930's.

studio was recognized almost immediately and became a main factor in the creation of a successful broadcast.

Radio stations, by May, 1922, totalled 314, creating a great number of difficulties. The problem of so rapidly expanding an industry became serious enough for President Warren G. Harding, in mid-winter, 1922, to instruct Secretary of Commerce Herbert Hoover to call a conference of manufacturers and broadcasters —the First National Radio Conference—in Washington. Secretary Hoover declared that the country was on the threshold of a new means of widespread communication which would have profound importance from the point of view of public education and welfare.

The conference accomplished a number of important results, which included the establishment of a Federal legal authority to control all transmitting stations except amateur and experimental stations. It also revealed that radio communication was to be considered a public utility and as such should be regulated by the Federal Government in the public interest.

Despite the fact that the first sponsored program had been made in August, 1922, few radio stations throughout the United States had hit upon a method by which money could be made, other than through the sale of radio equipment. Most American radio station operators found great difficulty in maintaining the cost of radio broadcasting. England solved the problem in 1922 by creating a government-controlled monopoly of broadcasting supported by taxes levied annually on each radio set. However, such a solution was considered impossible in the United States and serious difficulties were encountered by station broadcasters. Within the next few years, administrators in the broadcasting industry realized that only through sponsored programs could radio survive and flourish, giving birth to one of the greatest advertising media in the world.

T. J. Vastine conducted radio's first band concert over KDKA in 1921.

This sumptuous indoor tent studio was installed in a Pittsburgh Westinghouse plant in 1921. One of radio's first on-the-air mishaps occurred here, when a stray dog knocked over a microphone and added his loud barks to the ensuing pandemonium.

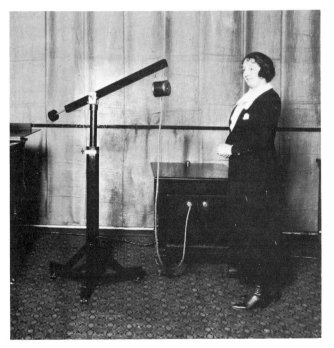

This 1921 picture shows an early microphone with a boom arrangement that permitted it to be raised or lowered according to the performer's height.

Other stations used the tent-studio idea to combat echo. Here is RCA's first broadcasting studio at Roselle Park, New Jersey, in 1921.

The Aeriola, Jr., got heavy use in the early 1920's. Rural listeners particularly turned to their sets for farm information, weather reports, and even for church services.

The original crew of WWJ is shown ready to go on the air in 1922, using the station's first transmitter. The horn type of microphone funneled the voice—or in this case the phonograph music—into the transmitter. Power was supplied by a 150-watt, 500-volt direct current generator driven by a quarter-horsepower motor placed under the table.

Will Rogers and a group of *Ziegfeld Follies* girls broadcast from the Pittsburgh *Post* studio of KDKA in 1922.

"The great commoner," William Jennings Bryan, broadcast a sermon from Point Breeze Presbyterian Church in Pittsburgh over KDKA in 1922.

Crystal sets were generally in use in 1922, requiring the listener to use earphones in order to hear the programs picked up. This contraption made it impossible for more than one person to listen in. Loudspeakers which could transmit the sound loud enough for groups of people had not yet been perfected. Considerable static in radio reception was also a tremendous problem at that time, and it was not until years later that solutions were discovered.

When Station WJZ was eleven months old in August, 1922, a young singer named Milton J. Cross was hired. His singing voice was ideal for broadcasting, but his speaking voice also won great acclaim and was destined to become one of the most familiar voices in radio. Another notable performer from the studios of WJZ in the spring of 1922 was Miss Bertha

*We two boys without a care*
*Entertain you folks out there—*
*That's our hap-hap-happiness!*

Billy Jones and Ernie Hare, radio's legendary "Happiness Boys," were perhaps the first of the broadcasting comedians to gain a wide audience.

Brainard, who made regular appearances in a series called "Broadcasting Broadway" in which she reviewed plays and offered other information about the theater.

During the same year, Gimbel Brothers' department store broadcast an hour-long musical program. The

American Tobacco Company came on the air and joined radio with its Lucky Strike Radio Show.

On August 22, 1923, the Happiness Candy Company went on the air with a new type of program. The show called "The Happiness Boys," featured Billy Jones and Ernie Hare, and provided a comparatively small audi-

Vladimir Rosing lets a song go out of his heart, apparently to a piano and phonograph accompaniment. The year is 1922.

Bertha Brainard, sometimes called the "First Lady of Radio," made regular appearances on WJZ in a program series called "Broadcasting Broadway," in which she reviewed plays and offered other information about the current theatre.

A young man named Milton Cross joined the staff of WJZ in 1922. Despite the fact that he made his debut as a tenor, he was hired as an assistant to Thomas H. Cowan, New York's first radio announcer. Cross, shown here in about 1928, was destined to become the nation's foremost commentator on musical programs, particularly the Metropolitan Opera broadcasts, with which his name is almost synonymous.

The nation's first full-time radio announcer was Harold W. Arlin of KDKA. Mr. Arlin spent five years behind the mike. During this period he introduced such public figures as William Jennings Bryan, Marshal Foch, and David Lloyd George. He also broadcast the first play-by-play account of a football game, between the University of West Virginia and the University of Pittsburgh.

ence with the first real comedy of radio. Utilizing a small studio so that the laughter would be heard on the air, "The Happiness Boys" helped to plunge the nation into a new era of radio programming.

Also in 1923 Roxy (S. L. Rothafel) and His Gang began their Sunday morning broadcasts from the Capitol Theater in New York, a series that was to continue, in only slightly altered form, into the late 1930's as The Capitol Theater Family with Roxy's successor, "Major" Edward Bowes.

One of radio's most beloved figures, Dr. Walter Damrosch, who would play an incalculable role in the popularization of serious music in America, made his first air appearance on October 29, 1923, with a lecture recital on Beethoven, over WEAF.

A young man named Graham McNamee made his debut that year, too. McNamee, who was more notable for his ability to project the atmosphere and excitement of a sports event into the nation's living rooms than for his reporting accuracy, became one of the

most popular announcers in early radio. Together with Phillip Carlin, he covered most of the important sports events of a decade and more.

WEAF, WCAP, and WJAR provided the vehicle for a number of important personages: David Lloyd George, Prime Minister of Great Britain on a goodwill tour to the United States, made an important broadcast. Ex-President Woodrow Wilson broadcast a ten-minute message to the country on the significance of Armistice Day. The first broadcast of a football game was made by Graham McNamee at the annual Army-Navy event.

Republicans gathered in Cleveland on June 10, 1924 for a three-day national convention. It was the first convention to be broadcast to the American people. When Graham McNamee and Major John Andrew White reported in vivid language the exciting Coolidge "bandwagon" scene, millions of listeners were experiencing history in the making.

Later in 1924, when 1,444 delegates assembled in

Frank E. Mullen, a Sioux City Farm editor, broadcast a regular farm program on KDKA in 1921.

Helen Hahn, one of the first radio hostesses and woman announcers, was heard over WBAY in New York.

Madison Square Garden, New York City, the American radio audience was able to listen in on the Democratic National Convention.

A typical program of 1924 is reproduced below. This WEAF program log records an interesting mixture of sustaining and sponsored offerings.

PROGRAM—Friday, September 12, 1924
Station WEAF—American Telephone and
Telegraph Company
(492 Meters 610 Kilocycles) (Daylight Saving Time)
195 Broadway, New York City

| | |
|---|---|
| 11:00 a.m. | Helen Morris, Soprano. |
| 11:10 a.m. | Health Talk under the auspices of the Association for the Prevention and Relief of Heart Disease, by Dr. Wm. St. Lawrence. |
| 11:25 a.m. | "The Flower Garden's Big Opportunity" by Leonard Barron, Editor of *Garden Magazine and Home Builder*. |
| 11:50 a.m. | Consolidated Market and Weather Reports by the United States Department of Agriculture and the New York State Department of Farms and Markets, together with *American Agriculturist*. |
| 4:00-5:00 p.m. | "Women's Club Program." |
| 4:00 p.m. | John Burnham, Concert Pianist, Program: "The Harmonious Blacksmith" (Handel); First Movement "Sonata" (Beethoven); "By the Brook" (Boisdefre). |
| 4:10 p.m. | Talk by Mr. Arthur J. Westermayr. |

| | |
|---|---|
| 4:25 p.m. | John Burnham, Concert Pianist, Program: "Waltz" (Chopin). |
| 4:35 p.m. | "When Every Voter Votes," the second in a series of lectures on "Getting Out the Vote" by Mrs. Raymond Brown, Managing Director of Woman's Citizen, speaking under the auspices of the New York League of Women Voters. |
| 4:50 p.m. | John Burnham, Pianist. Program: "Impromptu" and "Gavotte Antique" (compositions by Mr. Burnham). |
| 6:00 p.m. | Dinner Music from the Rose Room of the Hotel Waldorf-Astoria, New York City, Joseph Knecht, directing. Program: "Marche Lorraine" (Ganne); Selection "Les Huguenots" (Meyerbeer); "Arlesienne" (Bizet); "Caprice Viennois" (Kreisler); Entr'acte and Valse from "Coppelia" (Delibes); "Habañera" (Chabrier); "Lob der Frauen" (Strauss); "Madame Sherry" (Hoshna). |
| 7:30 p.m. | "Sir Hobgoblin Broadcasts a Get-Up-Time-Story" by Blanche Elizabeth Wade, the G. R. Kinney and Company Story Teller. |
| 7:45 p.m. | Harry Jentes, Jazz Pianist. |
| 7:55 p.m. | Rosella Sheiner, 10-year-old Violinist. |
| 8:05 p.m. | Isabel Duff "Scotty" Wood, Soprano, Program of Scotch Songs. |
| 8:20 p.m. | Harry Jentes, Jazz Pianist. |
| 8:35 p.m. | Joseph White, Tenor, Accompanied by Winifred T. Barr. |
| 8:50 p.m. | Rosella Sheiner, 10-year-old Violinist. |
| 9:00-10:00 p.m. | B. Fischer and Company's "Astor Coffee" Dance Orchestra. |

Joseph M. White, the "Silver Masked Tenor," was heard over WEAF in New York from 1923 to 1927 as soloist with the Goodrich Silvertown Orchestra. His identity was carefully guarded, and he wore a sterling silver mask when he appeared in public. He signed an exclusive contract with NBC in 1929 and was heard regularly until 1940, when he retired after sustaining serious injuries in an automobile accident. He died in 1959.

| | |
|---|---|
| 10:00 p.m. | Joseph White, Tenor. |
| 10:15-11:00 p.m. | Special Radio Program on National Defense. Test Day direct from the War Department Building, Washington, D.C. Speeches by General J. J. Carty, Hon. John W. Weeks, Secretary of War, and General John J. Pershing, General of the Armies of the United States and Chief of Staff, in order named. |

The summer of 1924 also saw a continuance of the controversy regarding the question of financial support of radio broadcasts. Secretary of Commerce Herbert Hoover expressed the opinion that broadcasting should be supported by industry. H. B. Thayer, president of the American Telephone and Telegraph Company, solved the company's problem by selling time on all its broadcasting stations. David Sarnoff, vice-president and general manager of the Radio Corporation of America, advocated outright endowment of radio broadcasting stations. He argued that because radio had reached the stage where it actually contributed a

An afternoon religious service broadcast by KDKA in 1923.

great deal to the happiness of mankind it deserved endowments similar to those enjoyed by libraries, museums and educational institutions. For the General Electric Company, Martin P. Rice stated that broadcasting should be supported by voluntary contributions or by licensing individual radio sets.

Since little money was available, few performers were paid for their services. The great newspaperman Heywood Broun, in protest, described the plight of the unpaid artist and predicted that this situation would be solved by some sort of financial support by advertisers.

The impact of radio in this country was so great that it had become one of the most influential forces in American life, stimulating every phase of activity.

Calvary Episcopal Church, Pittsburgh, was the scene of the first regularly scheduled church broadcasts, January, 1921.

The first portable radio? This perambulator-borne set may be it. Apparently people without babies could substitute dolls, as this young lady has done.

New stars were born, new expressions were popularized as new program formats were being offered. Radio was penetrating every third home in the country, and tenement house roofs were covered with forests of antennae.

Politically too, radio was making its mark. When after Harding, President Calvin Coolidge delivered his message to Congress, for the first time, people of the Nation had an opportunity to listen to this important event. Undoubtedly radio played a vital role in the career of Calvin Coolidge and helped to re-elect him in 1923.

His inauguration was covered by radio on March 4th, 1925, by 21 stations from Boston to San Francisco, under the banner of the AT&T network. It was estimated that fifteen million people listened to the voice of the President on this occasion.

This same year saw the appearance of John McCormack, the famous Irish tenor on WEAF, and of Lucrezia Bori of the Metropolitan Opera Company. This was the first in a series of broadcasts of great figures in the music world who had not previously been heard on radio because of the fear that broadcasting would adversely affect the sales of their recordings made for the Victor Talking Machine Company. A sustaining program of grand opera followed, with five stations participating in the broadcast. The program was so successful that a radio opera company was organized under the name of "The WEAF Grand Opera Company" and directed by Cesare Sodero.

1925 also saw the emergence of new radio personalities. The "A & P Gypsies" were delighting listening audiences on six stations, the "Gold Dust Twins"

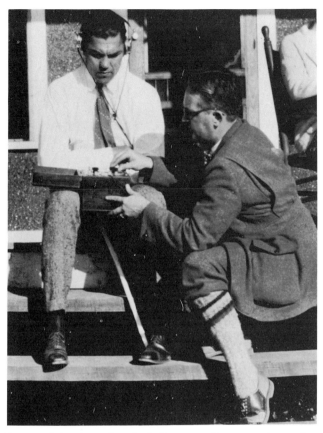

Heavyweight champion Jack Dempsey listens to the radio music box, tuned in by Major J. Andrew White, a pioneer announcer. This took place at Dempsey's training quarters a few days before the Dempsey-Carpentier fight in 1921.

Actress Olga Petrova appeared before the microphone in costume, as many performers in radio would later do.

**Daily Schedule Is Announced for Radio Broadcast**

Oct 9 - 1921

FOR the information of those who already have receiving sets or those who may install them during the week, following is the time schedule of the numbers on the daily broadcasting schedule:

1:45 P. M.—World Series, play by play.

8:05 P. M.—Baseball comment and an analysis of the World Series game.

8:15 P. M.—Summary of the day's important news dispatches.

8:30 P. M.—Concert program of musical and vocal selections.

On Friday night at 7 o'clock fairy stories told by The Man in the Moon and three musical numbers especially selected for children.

The sending of the World Series reports, of course, is governed by weather conditions. In the event that rain may prevent the game taking place, announcement of that fact will be made at several intervals during the afternoon.

A daily schedule from a newspaper of October 9, 1921.

Mobility was the thing in radio even in 1926. By that time KDKA had more than forty pick-up points in Pittsburgh, besides this car and crew which were used to cover special events.

A scene in KDKA's East Pittsburgh studios in 1925. The soloist (unidentified) was required to sing extremely loud in order to have her voice carry over the airwaves.

Borrowing prestige from the legitimate theatre, WJZ in 1923 broadcast *The Laughing Lady*, starring Ethel Barrymore, who was appearing in the same play on Broadway.

brought unique programs to the listeners of eight radio stations; the soft music of the Goodrich Silvertown Orchestra, and the singing voice of the Silver Masked Tenor, were a regular Thursday night transmission on WEAF. The famous Atwater Kent program was inaugurated in October of 1925, and brought the world's great musicians to the fast-growing radio audience. By this time, of course, the industry had succumbed

Harry B. Thayer, president of the American Telephone and Telegraph Company, speaks directly to England on January 14, 1923, over the first radio-telephone line.

*"One, two, three, four . . ."* KDKA began early-morning physical culture broadcasts in 1924. "Spike" Shannon was the instructor.

"The sweetest music this side of heaven." Guy Lombardo and his Royal Canadians were early performers on radio and one of the first orchestras to achieve national fame through this medium. Lombardo developed a sweet style of playing which has changed little through the years. For many people the New Year wouldn't seem official without Lombardo's "Auld Lang Syne."

to, and was flourishing on, the financial support of advertisers.

The extent of radio's success was feared by newspaper publishers throughout the country. The American Newspaper Publishers Association warned members that advertising on radio would result in a split in advertising appropriations and therefore would mean less revenue for newspapers. This fear was so great that many newspapers refused to carry radio logs in their papers, and the very word "radio" was forbidden in news columns. However, time proved this fear to be groundless and newspaper publishers gradually realized that radio had become an important supplemental medium, in many instances helping the newspaper industry to prosper.

America's first nation-wide network, the National Broadcasting Company, was born on November 15, 1926. The new network, with WEAF in New York as its key station, combined a group of nineteen scattered affiliated stations, using more than 3500 circuit miles of special telephone wires.

The Federal Radio Commission was appointed by President Coolidge on the basis of the Radio Act of 1927, which Congress passed in an effort to control broadcasting. A period of transition had ended and a new period of rapid development was born. In January of 1927, the first coast-to-coast program, originating in California, was broadcast. It was the Rose Bowl Football game and it was broadcast over the NBC network.

In 1927, radio took on larger dimensions for the American people. It was reaching greater distances at night, and the quality of programs was improving and their number increasing. A one-hour broadcast of Floyd Bennett's funeral service in Arlington held the nation spellbound. The voice of Herbert Hoover, accepting the Republican nomination from Palo Alto,

Thomas Alva Edison addresses the radio audience in 1926.

# Announcing the

# National Broadcasting Company, Inc.

National radio broadcasting with better programs permanently assured by this important action of the *Radio Corporation of America* in the interest of the listening public

THE RADIO CORPORATION OF AMERICA is the largest distributor of radio receiving sets in the world. It handles the entire output in this field of the Westinghouse and General Electric factories.

It does not say this boastfully. It does not say it with apology. It says it for the purpose of making clear the fact that it is more largely interested, more selfishly interested, if you please, in the best possible broadcasting in the United States than anyone else.

### Radio for 26,000,000 Homes

*The market for receiving sets in the future will be determined largely by the quantity and quality of the programs broadcast.*

We say quantity because they must be diversified enough so that some of them will appeal to all possible listeners.

We say quality because each program must be the best of its kind. If that ideal were to be reached, no home in the United States could afford to be without a radio receiving set.

Today the best available statistics indicate that 5,000,000 homes are equipped, and 21,000,000 homes remain to be supplied.

*Radio receiving sets of the best reproductive quality should be made available for all, and we hope to make them cheap enough so that all may buy.*

The day has gone by when the radio receiving set is a plaything. It must now be an instrument of service.

### WEAF Purchased for $1,000,000

The Radio Corporation of America, therefore, is interested, just as the public is, in having the most adequate programs broadcast. It is interested, as the public is, in having them comprehensive and free from discrimination.

Any use of radio transmission which causes the public to feel that the quality of the programs is not the highest, that the use of radio is not the broadest and best use in the public interest, that it is used for political advantage or selfish power, will be detrimental to the public interest in radio, and therefore to the Radio Corporation of America.

To insure, therefore, the development of this great service, the Radio Corporation of America has purchased for one million dollars station WEAF from the American Telephone and Telegraph Company, that company having decided to retire from the broadcasting business.

The Radio Corporation of America will assume active control of that station on November 15.

### National Broadcasting Company Organized

The Radio Corporation of America has decided to incorporate that station, which has achieved such a deservedly high reputation for the quality and character of its programs, under the name of the National Broadcasting Company, Inc.

### The Purpose of the New Company

*The purpose of that company will be to provide the best program available for broadcasting in the United States.*

The National Broadcasting Company will not only broadcast these programs through station WEAF, but it will make them available to other broadcasting stations throughout the country so far as it may be practicable to do so, and they may desire to take them.

*It is hoped that arrangements may be made so that every event of national importance may be broadcast widely throughout the United States.*

### No Monopoly of the Air

The Radio Corporation of America is not in any sense seeking a monopoly of the air. That would be a liability rather than an asset. It is seeking, however, to provide machinery which will insure a national distribution of national programs, and a wider distribution of programs of the highest quality.

*If others will engage in this business the Radio Corporation of America will welcome their action, whether it be cooperative or competitive.*

If other radio manufacturing companies, competitors of the Radio Corporation of America, wish to use the facilities of the National Broadcasting Company for the purpose of making known to the public their receiving sets, they may do so on the same terms as accorded to other clients.

The necessity of providing adequate broadcasting is apparent. The problem of finding the best means of doing it is yet experimental. The Radio Corporation of America is making this experiment in the interest of the art and the furtherance of the industry.

### A Public Advisory Council

In order that the National Broadcasting Company may be advised as to the best type of program, that discrimination may be avoided, that the public may be assured that the broadcasting is being done in the fairest and best way, always allowing for human frailties and human performance, it has created an Advisory Council, composed of twelve members, to be chosen as representative of various shades of public opinion, which will from time to time give it the benefit of their judgment and suggestion. The members of this Council will be announced as soon as their acceptance shall have been obtained.

### M. H. Aylesworth to be President

The President of the new National Broadcasting Company will be M. H. Aylesworth, for many years Managing Director of the National Electric Light Association. He will perform the executive and administrative duties of the corporation.

Mr. Aylesworth, while not hitherto identified with the radio industry or broadcasting, has had public experience as Chairman of the Colorado Public Utilities Commission, and, through his work with the association which represents the electrical industry, has a broad understanding of the technical problems which measure the pace of broadcasting.

One of his major responsibilities will be to see that the operations of the National Broadcasting Company reflect enlightened public opinion, which expresses itself so promptly the morning after any error of taste or judgment or departure from fair play.

*We have no hesitation in recommending the National Broadcasting Company to the people of the United States.*

*It will need the help of all listeners. It will make mistakes. If the public will make known its views to the officials of the company from time to time, we are confident that the new broadcasting company will be an instrument of great public service.*

## RADIO CORPORATION OF AMERICA

OWEN D. YOUNG, *Chairman of the Board*        JAMES G. HARBORD, *President*

This newspaper advertisement proclaimed the founding of NBC in 1926. It heralded the dawn of a new era in home entertainment and public service in broadcasting.

Here goes! Chief Engineer O. B. Hanson (*standing, right*) gives the signal to put the first NBC show on the air on November 15, 1926.

was a major radio event. Americans were listening to Moran and Mack, the "Two Black Crows," and sitting in rapt attention before their loud speakers for the Sunday afternoon broadcast of the Columbia Symphony Orchestra. Sponsors like Dodge, Listerine, Wrigley, and Studebaker were buying time on radio. By now there were eight million radio families in the country. This year, too, found such popular programs as that of Ida Bailey Allen and her cooking school. One of the country's popular radio personalities was an announcer named Ted Husing, whose specialty was sports events, but who doubled in anything that came along. It was Husing who broadcast the arrival of the *Graf Zeppelin* over New York in its first transatlantic flight. It was also Husing who made the memorable broadcast of the 1928 election returns.

During the same year, NBC was organized into two semi-independent networks, the Blue and the Red. The Blue Network consisted of WJZ and the older Radio Group Network. The Red Network encompassed WEAF and the older Telephone Group Network.

The Columbia Broadcasting System was founded in 1929, under the aegis of William S. Paley, the twenty-seven-year-old heir to a tobacco fortune. Paley

Veteran stage trouper Alice Brady faces a lamp shade that hides a microphone. Even experienced performers "froze up" when faced by a mike in 1926.

Vaughn de Leath is said to be the original "radio girl" and the first woman ever to have sung on the air. According to one story, Miss de Leath was invited into the original De Forest Laboratory, where she faced a phonograph horn. Then, it is said, she sang "The Old Folks at Home"—just for a lark. In any case, Vaughn de Leath, in the early 1920's, created the style of singing known as "crooning." Her style was imposed on her by the limitations of the radio equipment of the day, since the high notes of sopranos often blew out the delicate tubes of the transmitters. Ben Gross of the New York *Daily News* reported that "after her first broadcast, more than thirty years ago, Vaughn received one of the first radio fan letters ever written. It read: 'You have inaugurated a new form of song which, no doubt, will become very popular.'"

Miss de Leath also participated in the early NBC television broadcasts. Here she is on a novelty program in the late 1920's. She shares the camera with "Young Tarzan."

When CBS opened its new building at 485 Madison Avenue on September 18, 1929, President William S. Paley was on hand to supervise the ceremonial cutting of the ribbon.

had been greatly impressed by the boost in cigar sales as the result of a program broadcast over the almost-bankrupt Columbia Phonograph Broadcasting Company network. He merged the network with an organization called United Independent Broadcasters, which had been formed to supply talent for independent stations, and retained the Columbia name (although he sold the record company). The new network went on the air with 47 stations, with WABC (now WCBS) in New York as its key station. Interestingly enough, CBS in 1938 would repurchase the record company that gave it its name and build it up to the position of prestige it holds today.

The first sponsored opera broadcast originated from the stage of the Chicago Civic Auditorium in 1927. Cities Service, one of radio's oldest continuous sponsors, started its concert series in February of that year.

A major event of 1927 was the arrival of Charles A. Lindbergh in Washington, D.C., after his historic flight to Paris. The arrival was broadcast by Graham McNamee on a coast-to-coast network, with one of the greatest radio audiences in history listening in. The Dempsey-Tunney prizefight was broadcast from Chicago over 69 stations, the largest network of stations ever to carry a program to date. On November 7, General Motors began its first series on NBC, and the following month, the "Palmolive Hour" began.

In 1928, Al Jolson, already a star in other fields of entertainment, made his radio debut, and later that

Weber and Fields, vaudeville immortals, brought their act to radio in the early days.

Charles A. Lindbergh's solo flight across the Atlantic in May, 1927, was probably the event that more than any other epitomized the decade. "Lindy" was young, goodlooking, and daring—a made-to-order hero for a generation that reverenced these qualities above all others. The nation went wild when the news came that he had landed "The Spirit of St. Louis" safely outside of Paris and wilder still when he arrived home aboard a United States battleship. Graham McNamee was on hand in Washington to describe the hero's return to radio listeners. President Coolidge made him welcome in ceremonies broadcast from the foot of the Washington Monument. Later, Governor Alfred E. Smith of New York awarded him the State Medal in ceremonies held in Central Park.

In 1931, CBS awarded the aviator the Columbia Medal for Distinguished Service to Radio during a broadcast that was carried by the largest network of stations ever assembled up to that time.

Tragedy entered Lindbergh's life in 1932, when his infant son was kidnapped and later found dead. The picture shows a group of NBC newsmen making an on-the-spot broadcast in connection with the case.

Dr. S. Parkes Cadman, noted Brooklyn clergyman and nationally syndicated columnist, pioneered in a regular weekly religious series over NBC in 1928.

Microphones were getting fancy in the late 1920's and so were performers on radio, as more and more movie stars and Broadway actors tried the new medium.

Broadway showman S. L. Rothafel became well known to radio listeners as "Roxy." The famous Roxy Gang, broadcast from the Capitol Theatre in New York, was an NBC favorite for many seasons. Roxy gave the country such personalities as Erno Rapee, James Melton, "Wee Willy" Robyn, Caroline Andrews, and Marie Gambarelli.

year one of the first religious programs, the "National Radio Pulpit," became a network offering.

The broadcast coverage of the Republican Convention in June of 1928 was one of the most comprehensive ever attempted, and the Democratic Convention was covered to an equal extent during the same month. On August 6, one of the first dramatic series was begun. The program was called "Real Folks," and attained immediate popularity. The same year saw the inaugural programs of the "National Farm and Home Hour" and the "Music Appreciation Hour" with Dr. Walter Damrosch.

Radio listeners heard Herbert Hoover accept victory and Alfred E. Smith of New York concede defeat. Smith's "raddio" became a humorous expression throughout the country.

The "Voice of Firestone" began on December 24, and December 23 saw the inauguration of NBC's

Destined to become one of radio's brightest stars, lovely Jessica Dragonette gave up the concert stage for broadcasting. In the picture at the bottom Miss Dragonette appears on a Cities Service concert in the late 1920's. With her are conductor Rosario Bourdon and announcer Ford Bond (at microphone). When Jessica Dragonette retired from radio after a disagreement with her sponsors in the late 1930's, listeners were so distressed that in some cities fans resolved to boycott radio until she returned. During a concert tour 150,000 people turned out to hear her in Chicago's Grant Park, and in Minneapolis 15,000 people braved a blizzard and a taxi strike to hear her.

coast-to-coast network of 58 stations on a permanent basis.

1929 was also the year of Bing Crosby, of blindfold tests, and of Paul Whiteman. The La Palina Smokers' broadcast brought leading entertainers of stage and screen into America's living rooms. A CBS commenta-tor named H. V. Kaltenborn excited the public with his reports and analyses of major news events. This was the year that radio broadcast the ratification of the Kellogg-Briand Pact, and the short-wave flash of Byrd's flight over the South Pole.

The first short-wave broadcast from England was

The beloved Sir Harry Lauder was always a welcome guest in radio's first decade.

Herbert Hoover broadcast his acceptance of the Republican nomination for President in 1928. As Secretary of Commerce under Harding and Coolidge, Hoover played a large role in the early development of broadcasting.

made on February 1, with a program of symphonic music from Queen's Hall, London. Other "firsts" during this period included a regular weekly West-to-East program broadcast from San Francisco, the first airplane broadcast called "Over and Under New York," and the first re-broadcast from Sydney Australia. A parachute jumper broadcast his sensations as he floated down to earth one day in October. He was equipped for this NBC broadcast with a 25-pound, two-watt pack transmitter.

In the feverish autumn of 1929, the lugubrious strains of "A Perfect Song" every weekday evening announced "Amos 'n' Andy," and millions of listeners settled down for a much-needed laugh. Expressions

Graham McNamee interviews Babe Ruth during a game at Yankee Stadium.

Elsie Janis, vaudeville and Broadway star who became known as the "Sweetheart of the A.E.F." because of her indefatigable entertaining of the troops during World War I, made frequent radio appearances after the war. She was featured in several network productions, including "Hollywood on Parade."

History was made on February 2, 1929, when an NBC mobile unit brought voices from a plane in flight into the nation's living rooms.

Freeman Gosden ("Amos") and Charles Correll ("Andy") met in 1919 and formed a vaudeville team, doing a black-face act called "Sam 'n' Henry." They brought "Sam 'n' Henry" to Chicago radio in 1926 and in 1928 changed the act's name to "Amos 'n' Andy." Under the new name the show, which had been only moderately successful, became an immediate hit and in August of 1929 it went on the NBC network under the sponsorship of Pepsodent.

In the early days Gosden and Correll played all the roles on the program, but later other actors were added. The original team stills plays "Amos 'n' Andy" on radio, but other actors handle the roles on TV.

The tremendous and enduring popularity of "Amos 'n' Andy" was well deserved, for the program had real warmth and wit, and in such characters as the raffish "King Fish" and "Madame Queen" it presented some of the few truly original creations of radio comedy.

"The Rise of the Goldbergs" made its bow on NBC on November 20, 1929. Gertrude Berg, writer, producer, and star of the program, became so closely identified with the character she played that her friends called her "Molly." The Goldbergs continued their adventures on radio until 1946, and the show was revived on television in 1949. The roster of alumni of "The Goldbergs" is a distinguished one. Among the voices to be heard at one time or another on the show were those of Everett Sloane, Van Heflin, Joseph Cotten, Joan Tetzel, and Marjorie Main.

such as "I's regusted" and "check and double-check" made their way into the speech of the nation, and the trials and tribulations of Andy and the King Fish became popular topics of conversation.

Kate Smith, the "Songbird of the South," made the first appearance of her long radio career in 1929, and on a local station in Baltimore could be heard a young man who billed himself as Red Godfrey, the "Warbling Banjoist." (Radio in its early days made extensive use of descriptive sobriquets. There as Wendell Hall, the "Red-Headed Music Maker," Arthur Tracy, the "Street Singer," Ed Wynn, the "Fire Chief," Jan Garber, the "Idol of the Airlanes," Wayne King, the "Waltz King," and so on and on.)

Rudy Valley—he was the "Vagabond Lover"—kept millions of women virtually chained to their radios, from his opening "Heigh-ho, everybody" to the last nasal strains of "Your Time Is My Time." He and his Connecticut Yankees began their weekly broadcasts, called the "Fleischmann Hour," in October of 1929. He is often credited with being the originator of the radio variety show.

The 1920's saw the beginning of programming for children, with a host of imaginary "uncles" and "aunts" bringing entertainment to the nation's children. This trend was started by Don Carney and his "Uncle Don" program on WOR in New York. For almost twenty years his patter would change hardly at all. With parents sending him thousands of letters weekly, Carney could come up with such apparently omniscient items as this:

"Now today is the birthday of Willie Smith of Brooklyn, who has not been eating his vegetables the way he should. No he hasn't! And he ought to. But his Mama and Papa love him very much just the same, and if Willie will look behind the piano, I think he will find a present for his birthday."

Second only to "Uncle Don" in longevity was the celebrated CBS series, "Let's Pretend," a program produced and written by Lila Mack, on which children acted out stories.

Another early favorite was Irene Wicker, the "Singing Lady," who provided programs of nursery rhymes, interspersed with little skits and stories.

The early 1930's would see the rise of "radio clubs" with buttons, badges, secret signs and codes. Typical of these was "Chief Wolf Paw," with his password, "Ho-wah-ho-so-wah-ka." Another development of the 1930's was the amateur show, such as the "Horn & Hardart Children's Hour," and the "juvenile theatre," in which the children themselves participated. This was a format which attracted both children and their parents, and was therefore commercially very sound.

Dramatizations of comic strip characters, such as

Will Rogers became America's best-loved personality by dispensing his homespun philosophy and trenchant political observations on radio. Rogers was born in 1879 in Oklahoma. He spent his early years traveling in a wild west show, and made his first appearance on the vaudeville stage in New York, twirling a lariat. Subsequently he developed a humorous monologue and successfully performed in many Broadway shows. He became one of the great stars of the *Ziegfeld Follies,* and in 1918 began to appear in motion pictures. He published syndicated newspaper articles and frequently appeared on radio. Rogers was killed with Wiley Post in an airplane accident in 1935.

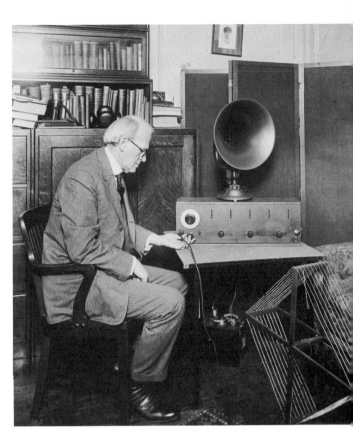

During the period from 1920 to 1930 the development of the radio receiver was phenomenal, as these three pictures, with only a few years between them, illustrate.

"Skippy" and "Little Orphan Annie" would prove tremendously successful in the 1930's. This was the era of the "box top thrillers," which combined an exciting story with the opportunity to get a free prize through the mail. All Junior had to do was see to it that Mom bought the sponsor's product.

Abuses crept into these programs. In an effort to retain audiences, the element of suspense was carried to extremes and there was often an excess of physical violence. Nationwide protest reached such proportions that Congress itself was moved to act, and bills were introduced designed to restrict the radio stations and networks in their programming for children.

Responding to the pressures, and in an effort to head off restrictive legislation, the networks promulgated their own codes for children's programs, eliminating "torture, horror, use of the supernatural or superstition likely to arouse fear" and banning profanity, vulgarity, kidnapping, and "cliff-hanging."

A program which adhered scrupulously to the code and yet achieved such popularity that it is probably the best-remembered of all children's serials was "Jack Armstrong, All-American Boy." When she heard its theme song ("Wave the flag for Hudson High, boys ..."), Mom knew that the kids were about to have a painless lesson in law and order, clean living, fair play, and good behavior.

Popular in the late 1930's and into the 1940's were such serials as "Buck Rogers," "Dick Tracy," "Captain Midnight" "Superman," and "The Lone Ranger."

The latter program, incidentally, was destined to make a peculiar contribution to American history. "Hi-yo, Silver!"—the "Lone Ranger's" familiar call to his horse—was actually used as a password by American troops entering Algiers during World War II.

Radio had taken root in the 1920's, and its branches rapidly expanded into all phases of American life. Both programming and listening during this decade were changing their patterns. Program personalities were beginning to attract loyal listeners. Obscure announcers and crooners became public heroes, to be idolized by millions of people who knew them only by voice.

The stock market crash and the subsequent depression were destined not to depress radio, but to add substantially to its ever-increasing audience. While movie houses closed, night clubs languished, and theatrical stock companies disappeared, radio boomed. Here was a medium of entertainment that was free, a mode of amusement provided to rich and poor alike without cost and in the privacy of the home. Thousands of families who had purchased much of their household equipment on credit gave up their vacuum cleaners, their cars, and their furniture, but kept up the payments on their radios. Radio had become a

part of their lives with which they could not part.

New national figures suddenly came into prominence. Radio philosophers arose who lectured to the millions on the ways of life and regularly received thousands of letters requesting help on personal problems. On the swelling tide of radio came scores of unemployed vaudeville and movie actors, night club performers, and concert stars to lend lustre and ingenuity to broadcasting. Advertisers, amazed by the huge audience, moved out of other media into radio, giving rise to a boom the like of which had never been experienced by any other industry. People loved radio and believed in it. Glued to their ever-more-elaborate sets, they were entranced by singing commercials, crooners, soap operas, mystery shows, comedians, quizzes—everything the magic box had to offer.

But there was criticism of the new medium, too.

Lee De Forest, speaking to a convention of broadcasters, cried out in dismay: "What have you done with my child [radio]? You have made him the laughing stock to intelligence, surely a stench in the nostrils of the gods of the ionosphere. Murder mysteries rule the waves by night and children are rendered psychopathic by your bedtime stories. This child of mine is moronic, as though you and your sponsors believe the majority of listeners have only moron minds."

Taking up the cry with De Forest were educators, sociologists and many government officials in the halls of Congress.

But the tide continued in the late twenties, and the industry was not to stop and take stock of itself until the 1930's, when mounting criticism caused the networks to set up their own codes of behavior and put forth increasing numbers of public service programs.

# Part Three: THE THIRTIES

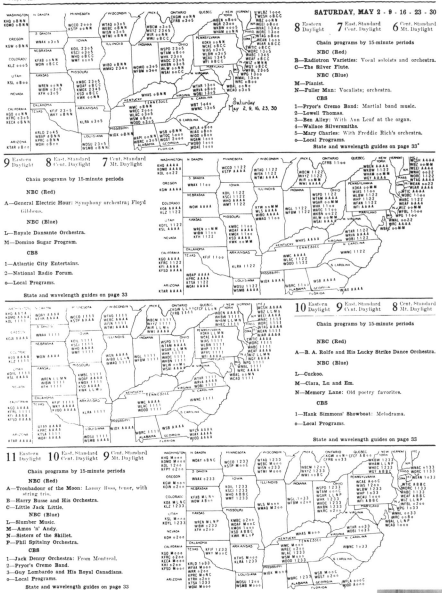

### SATURDAY, MAY 2 · 9 · 16 · 23 · 30

**8** Eastern Daylight    **7** East. Standard / Cent. Daylight    **6** Cent. Standard / Mt. Daylight

Chain programs by 15-minute periods

**NBC (Red)**
B—Radiotron Varieties: Vocal soloists and orchestra.
C—The Silver Flute.

**NBC (Blue)**
M—Pianist.
N—Fuller Man: Vocalists; orchestra.

**CBS**
1—Pryor's Cremo Band: Martial band music.
2—Lowell Thomas.
3—Ben Alley: With Ann Leaf at the organ.
4—Wallace Silversmiths.
5—Mary Charles: With Freddie Rich's orchestra.
o—Local Programs.
State and wavelength guides on page 33

---

**9** Eastern Daylight    **8** East. Standard / Cent. Daylight    **7** Cent. Standard / Mt. Daylight

Chain programs by 15-minute periods

**NBC (Red)**
A—General Electric Hour: Symphony orchestra; Floyd Gibbons.

**NBC (Blue)**
L—Royale Dansante Orchestra.
M—Domino Sugar Program.

**CBS**
1—Atlantic City Entertains.
2—National Radio Forum.
o—Local Programs.

State and wavelength guides on page 33

---

**10** Eastern Daylight    **9** East. Standard / Cent. Daylight    **8** Cent. Standard / Mt. Daylight

Chain programs by 15-minute periods

**NBC (Red)**
A—B. A. Rolfe and His Lucky Strike Dance Orchestra.

**NBC (Blue)**
L—Cuckoo.
M—Clara, Lu and Em.
N—Memory Lane: Old poetry favorites.

**CBS**
1—Hank Simmons' Showboat: Melodrama.
o—Local Programs.

State and wavelength guides on page 33

---

**11** Eastern Daylight    **10** East. Standard / Cent. Daylight    **9** Cent. Standard / Mt. Daylight

Chain programs by 15-minute periods

**NBC (Red)**
A—Troubadour of the Moon: Lanny Ross, tenor, with string trio.
B—Harry Busse and His Orchestra.
C—Little Jack Little.

**NBC (Blue)**
L—Slumber Music.
M—Amos 'n' Andy.
N—Sisters of the Skillet.
P—Phil Spitalny Orchestra.

**CBS**
1—Jack Denny Orchestra: From Montreal.
2—Pryor's Cremo Band.
3—Guy Lombardo and His Royal Canadians.
o—Local Programs.

State and wavelength guides on page 33

**What you could hear on a Saturday night in May, 1931.**

The radio had become the most imposing piece of furniture in the living room by 1931. This is a Stromberg-Carlson "console" of that year.

*"Nothing to fear but fear itself . . ."* More than any other, Franklin D. Roosevelt was the "radio President." His fireside chats, which he began eight days after his inauguration, inspired just the surge of confidence the nation needed in the dark days of the Depression. This was the first time the American people had been spoken to simply and directly by their President.

# The Thirties

The growth of radio networks in the late 1920's held tremendous implications for an American culture already in flux. The new medium united the far-flung cities of the nation as never before and brought the same entertainment to rural dwellers as to their city cousins, reaching deep into "pockets of culture" almost unchanged since the early nineteenth century. Thus radio continued the process of cultural homogenization already begun by the motion picture. By the end of the second decade of the twentieth century it was clear that American regionalism was dead.

Radio's spellbinding voice was heard everywhere, and its influence was felt in every phase of life. New expressions were popularized, new names became nationally famous, and new modes of eating, dressing, and thinking were almost hypnotically suggested by the voices from the box in the living room.

The development of radio programming proceeded at an uneven pace. The Federal Radio Commission, which in 1934 became the Federal Communications

Commission, moved in to clean up some of the programs which capitalized on the ills and misfortunes of mankind. Astrologers, fortune tellers, quack psychologists and doctors, such as the notorious John Romulus Brinkley, the "goat gland man," were taking to the airwaves in increasing numbers.

Network programming by 1930 had assumed the shape it would retain through the 1940's. Drama, comedy, music and news were timed to the split-second in quarter-, half-, and full-hour segments of the day. Because of the voracious appetite of the medium, talent and material were required in tremendous quantities. This gave rise to the syndication of scripts and recorded programs to local stations all over the country, resulting in a standardization of even non-network broadcasting.

The vast requirements of radio led to another development—the "packaged" show. Firms began to specialize in building and producing radio programs, which were delivered "complete" to the advertising agencies

Running over a tune with Alice Faye

The Vagabond Lover

On the air with Graham McNamee

"Heigh-ho, everybody!" Rudy Vallee and his Connecticut Yankees were probably the brightest stars in the radio firmament in the early 1930's. Vallee, a young New Englander, attended Yale and planned to teach. A mail-order course in the saxophone changed the course of his life. He formed a band and with his sax-playing and his nasal crooning became a great success in night clubs. On October 24, 1929, he began a series of weekly broadcasts called the "Fleischmann Hour" that would go on for a decade without change in sponsorship. It was probably radio's first really professional variety show. Among the songs identified with Vallee are "The Vagabond Lover," "Your Time is My Time," and the "Maine Stein Song."

Graham McNamee was announcer for early "Fleischmann Hour" broadcasts.

Irene Bordoni looks out from the cover of a popular radio magazine in 1931. Miss Bordoni, a star of the musical stage and screen, was appearing that year as "The Coty Play-girl" in her first radio series, complete with orchestra conducted by Eugene Ormandy. She was quoted in the magazine as saying, "I hope zat ra-deo will like me in ze same beeg way I like ra-deo." Radio did.

Baby Rose Marie, the "five-year-old child wonder," as her press agent called her, was radio's first child star.

and sold to clients. All elements were included in the "package," talent, script, sound effects, and production, absolving the networks of any need to create at all. Mass production had come to radio, and the networks would wake up one day to discover that they had all but lost control of what went out over their wires.

The result of program packaging, from the standpoint of the listener, was that radio offerings were indeed beginning to sound "stamped out." Hundreds upon hundreds of programs were being turned out with a regularity that all but assured sameness. Originality was, in fact, frowned upon, since it involved risk, and program quality was kept within rigid bounds, lest a too-good show should overshadow the "brief message from our sponsor."

The overall pattern of radio was set, and would remain essentially unchanged until the advent of tele-

vision jolted the medium out of its complacency.

But the 1930's found radio booming. Though there were rumblings of dissatisfaction from many quarters, "Mr. and Mrs. America" liked what they heard in the comfort of their living room.

In a 1933 issue of *Broadcasting* Magazine, L. B. Wilson, then managing director of a chain of theatres in Kentucky, wrote: "Radio is successfully competing with the theatre. Hard times have added millions of persons to the radio audience while taking millions from the theatre audience. You can get Eddie Cantor on the air for nothing. It costs you 50¢ or more to get him at the theatre."

Established stars of the theatre began to recognize the tremendous power of radio and were gradually moving over into the new medium. At first legitimate theatre actors and Hollywood stars had frowned upon radio as beneath their dignity, but as the number of radio receivers in the United States increased into the millions, these very same performers changed their views. It is said that Ethel Barrymore, who broke the "rule" and appeared on radio, opened the way for other stars. Certainly the fact that radio was creating its own stars who threatened to outshine those of

Ford Bond, right, and Graham McNamee beside him broadcasting a baseball game in the early 1930's.

Cooking expert Ida Bailey Allen in the early 1930's.

Broadway and Hollywood must have played a part in this change of attitude.

Many cultural programs gained new prestige and, sometimes, sponsors. The NBC Symphony Orchestra and the New York Philharmonic-Symphony were broadcasting regularly in the early 1930's, and before the decade was out, the Saturday afternoon broadcasts from the Metropolitan Opera would be inaugurated.

In March, 1930, a two-way conversation was made via radio between NBC officials and Admiral Byrd, the Antarctic explorer, after his arrival in New Zealand. Four days later, the first broadcast was made from a ship at sea to listeners on shore.

The "American School of the Air," an educational program especially designed to be heard in the nation's schoolrooms, was begun in 1930.

"The American School of the Air" on CBS was an early and highly successful attempt to make use of radio's educational potential. This picture shows a class listening to the program in about 1934.

"*Hear ye, hear ye!*" Alexander Woollcott as the Town Crier presented a program unique in broadcasting—an odd mixture of gossip and great literature.

Listeners who tuned in Monday nights heard a new voice, one imbued with the speed and staccato quality of a tommy-gun. This was Walter Winchell's first year of broadcasting the news and gossip of the Broadway scene—a coverage that would eventually be broadened to include the whole world. Alexander Woollcott, with his curious mixture of ascerbity and maudlin sentimentality, began his tremendously popular "Town Crier" broadcasts that year, and the Crossley report, one of radio's first rating systems, came into use.

People who were uneasy about the power of radio found new grounds for worry in the meteoric rise of Father Charles E. Coughlin of Royal Oak, Michigan, who captured the imagination of millions of Americans in the dark years of the Depression with his vague talk of "social justice."

During the month of April, a conversation between Marconi, aboard his yacht off the west coast of Italy, and NBC officials in New York was broadcast—foreshadowing the globe-hopping radio would do in the decades to come.

The arrival of the *Graf Zeppelin* at Lakehurst, New Jersey, was broadcast on May 31. In June plans were announced for a $250,000,000 Radio City to be built by John D. Rockefeller in New York. The 70-story RCA Building at its core would be the home of the National Broadcasting Company.

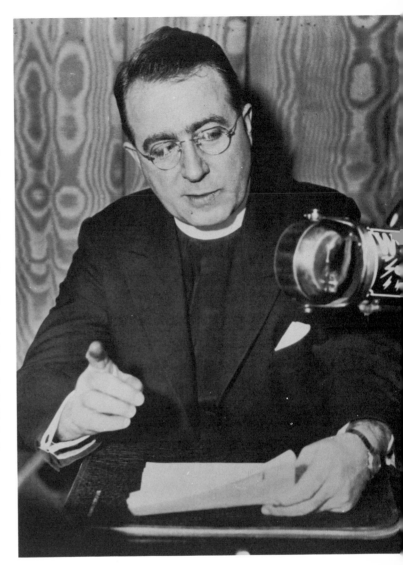

The Depression year of 1930 was a bleak one in the United States and all signs pointed to a worsening of conditions. So it is perhaps not surprising that the mellow, brogue-touched voice of Father Charles E. Coughlin coming from the radio loudspeaker, now lulling with visions of a better future, now lashing out at the "money-changers" and the Communists, should have captured first the attention, and then the loyalty, of millions of Americans.

All through the early 1930's Father Coughlin maintained a huge and highly responsive audience, estimated at anywhere from 30,000,000 to 45,000,000 and letters poured into his Shrine of the Little Flower at Royal Oak, Michigan, at the rate of 50,000 a week.

When CBS refused to renew his contract in 1933 (because he would not submit his speeches in advance), Coughlin returned to the air over an even larger network of stations, the time paid for by listener contributions. In 1934 he founded the National Union for Social Justice, an organization with a platform of high-sounding generalities (a "just, living, annual wage for all labor," etc.). Now the radio priest withdrew his support for Roosevelt's New Deal

and shifted from pro-labor unionism to open criticism of the unions.

By 1936 Coughlin was denouncing Roosevelt as a "scab president" and the "great betrayer and liar." Adherence to the World Court would be "treason." That year Father Coughlin formed the "Union Party" with its own Presidential candidate.

Slowly the tide was turning against him, though. He was under constant attack from Catholic leaders, including high churchmen like Cardinals O'Connell of Boston and Mundelein of Chicago, and laymen such as Al Smith. His Union Party suffered a resounding defeat in the elections of 1936. And in 1937 he was rebuked by his immediate superior, the new Archbishop of Detroit. The Holy See, through the Apostolic Delegate in America, saw fit to approve the Archbishop's action. As the radio priest's preachings became more rancorous, men of good will were turning away from him.

Coughlin lingered on until 1940. In April of that year his golden voice disappeared forever from the airwaves, his followers no longer able to afford his radio time.

As a popular CBS announcer, Floyd Gibbons delivered stories on the air at the speed of 217 words a minute and pioneered on-the-spot remote broadcasting. Handsome, rugged, and over six feet tall, Gibbons always wore a white patch over his left eye, which he had lost during the battle of Belleau Woods during World War I. Later, on NBC, he did a series called "Headline Hunters," telling exciting stories of his own adventures.

An early favorite was Norman Brokenshire, who developed a new style of broadcasting with his mellow voice and intimate delivery. A famous story is told of Brokenshire's quick thinking. His script ran short on one of his broadcasts, so he ad-libbed as long as he could. Finally, in desperation, he said, "Ladies and gentlemen, the sounds of New York!" and held the mike out the studio window.

The light Irish tenor of Morton Downey began to be heard on radio around 1929.

Tony Wons, with his close-to-the-mike technique, fluttered feminine hearts from coast to coast when he read poetry to them on "Tony Wons' Scrapbook," a popular morning program in the 1930's.

Floyd Gibbons was probably the most popular news broadcaster on the air at this time. But one night in 1930 a young man named Lowell Thomas substituted for him. The audience response to Thomas was so good that he was quickly hired to do a regular broadcast, and in the next quarter of a century would be a fixture on radio.

Fred Allen, one of radio's greatest comedians, made his broadcast debut as a guest on November 30. On December 11, NBC broadcast the arrival of Albert Einstein in New York.

Twenty-three new radio stations were authorized by the Federal Radio Commission in 1931, and the world's tallest skyscraper, the Empire State Building, was selected this same year to be the city's television transmitter. 125-line television transmission was developed and started by NBC.

On October 12, the "American Album of Familiar Music" began on NBC. By December of this year, two out of every five United States households owned radios. The United States Census Bureau reported over 12 million radio families in the country. It is interesting to note that during this period more than half the

The "Cliquot Club Eskimos," under Harry Reser's direction, made up a lively orchestra which specialized in musical sleighbells. Members of the group included Raymond Knight, Merle Johnston, Jimmy Brierly and Everett Clark.

Charles Winninger became known as "Captain Henry" to radio audiences as he piloted the "Maxwell House Show Boat," starting in 1929. Lanny Ross was also starred on the show.

Lou Holtz, one of vaudeville's greatest story-tellers, made frequent appearances on radio during the 1930's, regaling listeners with his tales of "Sam Lepidus."

With Leopold Stokowski

On the "Kate Smith Hour" during World War II

With Jack Miller (on podium) and David Ross (in white tie).

*"Hello, everybody!"* Thus melodious Kate Smith opened her tremendously popular broadcasts. "The Songbird of the South," as she was called, started her radio career in 1929 after having appeared as a comedienne and singer in *Honeymoon Lane* and other Broadway musicals. Her broadcasting career was carefully guided by her friend and manager, Ted Collins. Next to her famous signature song "When the Moon Comes Over the Mountain," Kate Smith is probably most closely identified with the wartime "God Bless America," written by Irving Berlin.

CBS covers the 1932 election returns. To the right of the pillar is H. V. Kaltenborn.

"Hello, Momma?" Never precisely a radio star, George Jessel was nevertheless familiar to millions of listeners who loved his telephone conversations with his doting Momma.

Mellow-voiced Boake Carter became a news commentator in 1930. In 1932 his meticulously accurate coverage of the Lindbergh kidnapping case for CBS skyrocketed him to fame.

nation's stations were operating without profit, maintaining their operations in the hope of future rewards.

In 1931, too, radio listeners heard Benito Mussolini declare that he had no designs on other countries, nor any desire to start war. They heard also the first world-wide broadcast of Pope Pius XI. Gertrude Ederle reported, via radio that year, how it felt to speak from an aquaplane. William Beebe made a radio

Fred Allen's first radio show, "The Linit Bath Club Revue," made its debut on October 23, 1932. His last show, "The Fred Allen Show," bowed out on June 26, 1949. Between those dates Allen gave the nation the most literate comedy radio had to offer. "Town Hall Tonight" is probably the program title people think of when they think of Allen, but it was on the "Texaco Star Theatre" in 1942 that he first strolled down "Allen's Alley" and met "Senator Claghorn" (Kenny Delmar) "Titus Moody" (Parker Fennelly), "Mrs. Nussbaum" (Minerva Pious), and "Ajax Cassidy" (Peter Donald).

Two feuds marked his radio career. One was a very real one with network officials, to whom Allen's nonconformism was galling. This led to his show being cut off the air at midpoint on at least one occasion. Following is the offending dialogue (with Portland Hoffa):

PORTLAND: Why were you cut off last Sunday? [The show had run overtime, as it often did.]

ALLEN: Who knows? The main thing in radio is to come on time. If people laugh, the program is longer. The thing to do is to get a nice dull half-hour. Nobody will laugh or applaud. Then you'll aways be right on time, and all of the little emaciated radio, executives can dance around their desks in interoffice abandon.

PORTLAND: Radio sure is funny.

ALLEN: All except the comedy programs. Our program has been cut off so many times the last page of the script is a Band-Aid.

Fred and his wife, Portland Hoffa, in 1932.

The Benny-Allen feud—a highly-posed tableau. Left to right, Portland, Jack Benny, Fred Allen, and Mary Livingstone, Benny's wife.

PORTLAND: What does the network do with all the time it saves cutting off the ends of programs?

ALLEN: Well, there is a big executive here at the network. He is the vice-president in charge of "Ah! Ah! You're running too long!" He sits in a little glass closet with his mother-of-pearl gong. When your program runs overtime he thumps his gong with a marshmallow he has tied to the end of a xylophone stick. *Bong!* You're off the air. Then he marks down how much time he's saved.

PORTLAND: What does he do with all this time?

ALLEN: He adds it all up—ten seconds here, twenty seconds there—and when he has saved up enough seconds, minutes, and hours to make two weeks, the network lets the vice-president use the two weeks of *your* time for *his* vacation.

PORTLAND: He's living on borrowed time.

ALLEN: And enjoying every minute of it.

The other "feud," with his good friend Jack Benny, was a publicity gag, but it aroused such listener interest in the late 1930's that when the two met on Benny's show March 14, 1937, purportedly to do physical battle with each other, radio survey figures showed that only one of FDR's fireside chats had ever drawn a larger audience. There was such a demand for tickets to the broadcast that it had to be held in the ballroom of the Hotel Pierre in New York.

A script session in 1947. That's Allen at the left and Harry Von Zell in the center. Allen wrote most of his material himself and all of it bore the stamp of his personality.

broadcast from a steel "Bathysphere," 2200 feet below sea level off the coast of Bermuda.

Floyd Gibbons' famous broadcast from the battlefields of Manchuria in 1932 stirred millions of Americans. On January 31, 1932, the World Disarmament Conference at Geneva, Switzerland, was broadcast to countries all over the world. In February, vocalist Jane Froman began a series which established her as a major entertainer in radio. March found radio emerging as an important news source with its extensive coverage of the kidnapping of Charles A. Lindbergh, Jr., including hourly bulletins on the development of the case.

"One Man's Family" began its long career in April, and on May 2, Jack Benny performed in his first program on radio after having abandoned a successful stage career. Jack Pearl emerged as a major radio personality in the character of "Baron Munchausen." October 6 saw the opening of the popular program, "Captain Henry's Maxwell House Show Boat," starring Charles Winninger, Lanny Ross, Jewels Bledsoe, Annette Hanshaw and many others, and on November 28 Groucho Marx delighted the radio audience with a new form of fast-moving comedy.

An excellent picture of radio in 1932 can be gotten

Don McNeill's "Breakfast Club," with its unashamed cornball humor, began in the early 1930's, and is still entertaining early-morning listeners as this book goes to press. McNeill is in profile in the center.

The all-star cast of Chesterfield's "Music That Satisfies" in 1932. The announcer is Norman Brokenshire. In group, clockwise from top, are Ruth Etting, Arthur Tracy, the "Street Singer," the Boswell Sisters, and Nat Shilkret.

from this "perfect program" as envisioned by Ring Lardner in that year:

*Announcer:* "This is Station WENC and the following program is sponsored by Fleischmann's Antiseptic Cigarette Oil. It comes to you every Saturday night, just an hour before bedtime. The oil is probably as good as any other oil you can buy. We have made no test to prove that statement, but it sounds reasonable because the well we get it from looks almost exactly like all the other wells we ever saw, and we have seen our full quota of oil wells. Now our program will open with George Olsen's music and Miss Fanny Brice." (One minute.)

George Olsen's orchestra, without the "railroad effect" theme, plays some new stuff, including a comedy song, dialect if possible, to be sung by Miss Ethel Shutta. Miss Brice, with a straight man, does some dialogue written by someone who can write for Miss Brice. (Four minutes.)

Ohman and Arden, on two pianos, without an orchestra, playing early Gershwin or recent Schwartz or both. (Two minutes.)

Stoopnagle and Budd in dialogue that does not contain any reference to Stoopnocracy. (Two minutes.)

Ben Bernie's orchestra, with Ben singing a refrain and making a remark or two. (One minute.)

Jack Pearl and Cliff Hall doing the kind of stuff they did before they got to do the kind of stuff they got to doing. (Four minutes.)

The Revelers in a medley of songs intended for quartets. No trick song or comedy song such as What's-his-name

Groucho Marx made many memorable appearances on radio during the 1930's, but he never really clicked with a regular show of his own.

In 1945, with ten movie successes (as one of the Marx Brothers) under his belt, he made another unsuccessful attempt to enter radio. Undaunted by failure, he accepted an offer to do a one-shot radio marathon with Bob Hope. Groucho was supposed to trade prepared quips with Bob. The show went poorly until Hope accidently dropped his script. Groucho placed his foot firmly on the material, and when Hope could not retrieve it, the show continued on an ad-lib basis.

Groucho was doing the thing he knew best now—unrehearsed, unwritten humor. Howls of laughter came from the studio audience. Thousands of calls and wires flooded the network. In the audience was a young producer, John Guedel, who went backstage to meet Groucho and propose a new show called "You Bet Your Life." It was this show that made Groucho Marx a radio (and subsequently a TV) star. (See page 145.)

Fanny Brice entered radio in the early 1930's and became popular as "Baby Snooks." Considered one of the great comediennes of her day, Miss Brice started her career as a song sheet illustrator. Later she was hired by George M. Cohan and Sam H. Harris as a singer and dancer. When she was seventeen, she was engaged by Florenz Ziegfeld for his "Follies," in which she achieved stardom singing "My Man." As "Snooks" on the radio Fanny Brice sorely tried the patience of her long-suffering Daddy, played for many years by Hanley Stafford.

A sample of "Baby Snooks" dialogue:

BRICE: Daddy.
FATHER: What?
BRICE: Is this Miss Gooseberry's school?
FATHER: Snooks, the lady's name is not Gooseberry. Its Shrewsbury, and they want you to be very careful while you're inside. Miss Shrewsbury doesn't admit every little girl. There are 110 students in her private school.
BRICE: That ain't so private.
FATHER: Snooks, we speak of a private school as opposed to a public school, which admits anyone. A public school has a large body of students. Miss Shrewsbury has a small body.
BRICE: Is she a midget?
FATHER: No, she happens to be a very cultured and dignified lady.

BRICE: Who?
FATHER: Who have we been talking about?
BRICE: Miss Gooseberry.
FATHER: *Shrewsbury!*

*"Vass you dere, Sharlie?"* Jack Pearl as Baron Munchausen, achieved great popularity in the early 1930's.

Jack Pearl with Cliff Hall.

Standing at the right of this photo from the early 1930's are Dr. Frank Black and tenor James Melton. The other men in the picture are The Revelers, popular singing quarter of which Melton was a member. They are, from left to right, Wilfred Glenn (seated), Lewis James, and Elliott Shaw.

playing the rumba on his tuba or any song in which the melody is sung by the bass. (Two minutes.)

Joe Cook, giving directions on how to get to his old home in Evansville from the C. & E. I. station. (Five minutes.)

Bing Crosby in a couple of his specials, with a good orchestra such as Denny's or Goodman's or Lopez's for him to fight it out with. (Four minutes.)

Ed Wynn, with Graham McNamee and Vorhees' band, telling some of those jokes it takes him thirty-one hours

Bing Crosby with the late Bob Burns on the "Kraft Music Hall."

A young Bing with the Boswell sisters in 1932.

Bing Crosby started out in life to be a lawyer and ended as the most famous popular singer of the twentieth century. His "Where the Blue of Night Meets the Gold of the Day" signature tune has been familiar on radio since the early 1930's, and his long series of hit motion pictures and fantastically successful recordings have made him a favorite in every corner of the world.

His greatest radio program, probably, was the famous "Kraft Music Hall" of the late 30's and early 40's. This was a relaxed hour-long variety show, with Bob Burns, John Scott Trotter's orchestra, special guests, and announcer Ken Carpenter. Both Trotter and Carpenter, incidentally, have been closely identified with Crosby ever since.

In 1960 Bing Crosby returned to radio after a few years' absence to do a Monday-through-Friday morning show with Rosemary Clooney.

per week to write, and trying, as a stunt, not to use his favorite word for 1932-33—"underwear." (Ten minutes.)

Rosa Ponselle, singing an aria from the opera *Norma*. (Two minutes and a half.)

Irvin S. Cobb, waiting for them to stop laughing before he starts his first story. (Half a minute.)

Burns and Allen, with Guy Lombardo's orchestra. We are crowded for time, but Burns and Allen rate as much as Stoopnagle and Budd and shall have it. Miss Gracie, at my request is doing over twice as much singing as usual.

With John Scott Trotter in 1935.

Metropolitan Opera star Rosa Ponselle appeared on the Chesterfield "Music That Satisfies" show in the early 1930's. In this photo from 1934 are, left to right, Andre Kostelanetz, Miss Ponselle, Ford Frick and Grete Stueckgold.

Ruth Etting, as she appeared on the Chesterfield program in the early 1930's. One of the truly great stars of her day, Miss Etting made popular such songs as "Love Me or Leave Me," "Ten Cents a Dance," and "Mean to Me."

Mr. Lombardo, in the minute allotted to him, will attempt to have his strings and saxophones in tune with his saxophones and strings for at least one encounter. (Five minutes.)

Ruth Etting, queen of the torchers, singing, perhaps, Irving Berlin's old "Remember." (One minute.)

Eddie Cantor and James Wallington in dialogue written by someone who knows how to write for Eddie Cantor. (Two minutes.)

A fellow named Lawrence Tibbett, singing in English a song called "Bendemeer's Stream," or, in Italian, the aria in *Traviata* which Daddy sings to the girl and which is virtually a complete history of France up to the time the United States entered the World War. (Two minutes.)

Fred Allen and Roy Atwell, in dialogue written by Fred Allen for Fred Allen, and something nobody will admit having written for Mr. Atwell. (Two minutes.)

Al Jolsin in anything he wants to sing or say. (Two minutes.)

And the remaining eight minutes to the best band in the land, Marse Paul's, who, I hope, will give me all the "Music in the Air" and other recent Kern he can crowd into that all too brief period.°

° From *The Portable Ring Lardner*, The Viking Press, New York, 1946.

On the night of January 30, 1933, the radio audience heard that a man named Adolf Hitler had become Chancellor of Germany.

The 73rd Congress permitted the first radio broadcast from the floor of the House for its opening on

Eddie Cantor came to radio from the Broadway stage, where he starred in the *Ziegfeld Follies* and such musicals as *Kid Boots* and *Whoopee*. Cantor got into show business at the age of 16, when his impersonations won him first prize in an amateur contest at Miner's Bowery Theatre. He later worked as a singing waiter in a Coney Island saloon, and then in burlesque and vaudeville. He appeared on radio occasionally during his stage career, but from the early 1930's on, he devoted all his time to the new medium and movies.

Throughout the 1930's he was one of the top attractions in radio, and in many years was *the* top attraction. He took an especial pride in developing new talent; among his protégés were Bobby Breen, Deanna Durbin, and Dinah Shore. He also introduced Burns and Allen to the radio audience. Cantor was untiring in his charitable work, too, his most famous project, probably, being the "March of Dimes."

Cantor faces the mike in 1923.

With one of the Cantor show's most famous characters, Bert Gordon as the "Mad Russian." (1938)

Here is an exchange with Harry Von Zell, for many years his announcer:

VON ZELL: Eddie, I understand you're making a tour all the way to New York.

CANTOR: Yes, New York. I love to go down on the East Side and see the house where I was born. Do you know, Harry, they've put up a plaque on the door, and you should see the crowds passing by every day.

VON ZELL: What does the plaque say?

CANTOR: No vacancy!

VON ZELL: Oh, stop clowning, Eddie, I'm anxious to get started. What train are we going on?

CANTOR: Well, the train I'm trying to get tickets for leaves on track 8, 9 and 10.

VON ZELL: That must be a long train.

CANTOR: No, a woman engineer brought it in side ways.

Fun with Ted Husing.

Burns and Allen in 1934

In 1936

George Burns and Gracie Allen received their schooling in oldtime vaudeville. Gracie, the daughter of a stage hoofer, made her debut at the age of three. George entered show business as a small boy in a Gus Edwards vaudeville act. They met in 1922 and formed a team, with Gracie playing "straight man" to George. It wasn't until three years later that they realized it was Gracie who was getting the laughs.

Their first air show was in 1931, as guests on Eddie Cantor's program. Their audience appeal proved so great that they were signed for appearances on the Rudy Vallee and Guy Lombardo shows. 1932 found them signed for their own network program on CBS, and they were regulars on radio and television until Gracie's retirement in 1958.

The patient George, with his dry, rasping voice, and scatterbrained Gracie, with a logic all her own, were perfect foils for each other, and they had a large and very loyal following. When they made a running gag of Gracie searching for her lost brother, a nation-wide search for him ensued. In desperation, her real, unlost brother wired his sister from San Francisco: "Have gone into hiding. Can't you make a living any other way?" It isn't recorded how many write-in votes Gracie received in the Presidential elections of 1940, but she conducted a vigorous, if nonsensical, campaign for the office on the radio.

Here is an example of Burns and Allen humor, dating from the World War II period:

BILL GOODWIN: Well, tonight we find George and Gracie just leaving their neighborhood movie where they have been watching a romantic Charles Boyer picture. Gracie is still under the spell of her screen idol.

GEORGE: Gracie, could you walk a little faster?

GRACIE: If you wish, Charles.

GEORGE: Gracie, I'm George Burns, your husband—remember? I'm not Charles Boyer.

GRACIE: Oh. Well, that's life.

GEORGE: Come on. I want to stop in the cigar store.

GRACIE: My, I'll never get over the way Charles Boyer kissed Barbara Stanwyck. I wonder how it feels to be kissed like that.

GEORGE: As soon as we get home I'll show you.

GRACIE: Mama's little dreamer.

GEORGE: Never mind, never mind. Here's the cigar store. [*Door opens.*

STANLEY: Good evening, Mr. Burns.

GEORGE: Good evening, Stanley. Give me three Perfecto Royals, please.

STANLEY: Yes, sir. Why, hello, Mrs. Burns.

GRACIE: Hello, Stanley.

In 1938

Harry Von Zell as he appeared about 1930. A veteran announcer, Von Zell graduated to acting roles on the "Burns and Allen Show" and other programs.

STANLEY: My, you're looking positively radiant tonight. There's a sparkle in your eyes and a glow in your cheek that only a man could put there.

GRACIE: It was a man, Stanley.

STANLEY: Well, well—there must be more to Mr. Burns than meets the eye.

GEORGE: We've just been to see Charles Boyer.

STANLEY: Oh! Well, here are your cigars.

GRACIE: Oh, George, pay Stanley for these ten movie magazines, too.

GEORGE: Ten movie magazines?

GRACIE: They all have articles about Charles Boyer. [Door opens.

In the 1940's, with daughter Sandra and son Ronnie. Ronnie has since achieved great popularity through his appearances on the Burns and Allen television show.

BOLEY: Greetings, Stanley. 'Tis I—Bolingbroke.

STANLEY (disgusted): Hello, Cueball.

GRACIE: Well, hello, Mr. Bolingbroke!

BOLEY: Why, bless me, if it isn't the Burnses—both the lovely one and the other one. Well, well, this is a most fortuitous happenstance!

GRACIE: It is?

BOLEY: Yes, I have great news for you, dear lady! The Bolingbroke Little Theatre is about to open its winter theatrical season. I shall want you as the leading lady, naturally.

Gracie: Oh, naturally. Say, wouldn't it be wonderful if we could get Charles Boyer for my leading man?

GEORGE: Oh, sure, sure. You could get him easy for around twenty-five thousand dollars.

GRACIE: We wouldn't have to pay him a cent, George—he's Free French.

With Jerry Colonna, for years associated with the Bob Hope Show. (1938)

In the early 1940's, with friend Bing Crosby and Jerry Colonna . Hope and Crosby frequently visited back and forth on each other's shows.

Bob Hope entered radio in 1934. He came from the stage, where he had starred in the *Ziegfeld Follies* and in such shows as *Roberta*. Hope also toured the country in vaudeville. In 1938 he was signed for *The Big Broadcast of 1938,* which was followed by a series of successful films, including the famous "Road" series with Bing Crosby and Dorothy Lamour.

Hope's humor depends upon a rapid-fire delivery and is often topical in content. In fact, Hope is one of the few comedians who have achieved top positions in broadcasting who comments directly on the news of the day. Few listeners will ever forget the characters "Brenda and Cobina," who appeared on the Hope shows of the late 1930's and were hilarious spoofs of two popular debutantes of the era. Although he depends greatly on barbed remarks about other people, he doesn't mind being funny at his own expense.

Bob Hope's record of entertaining American troops during World War II and later is unmatched.

Some Hope humor:

HOPE: You're a small girl, Ida. You hardly come up to my chin.
IDA: Which one?
HOPE: Those aren't chins. That's a staircase for my Adam's Apple.

An exchange with comedienne Vera Vague:

HOPE: Oh, girl jockeys are nothing new, Miss Vague. After all, there was Lady Godiva.
VERA: Lady Godiva?
HOPE: Yeah, the original Gypsy Rose Lee.
VERA: Lady Godiva never won a horse race, did she?
HOPE: No, Miss Vague, she just showed.

March 9. On March 12, President Roosevelt addressed the nation in his first "Fireside Chat," explaining to the country the reasons for his historic bank moratorium.

The attempted assassination of President Roosevelt in Miami received prompt and vast coverage. CBS put eye-witnesses on the air within 90 minutes of the occurrence, via a special line. On March 15 the largest audience in history listened to President Roosevelt's plans to reopen the nation's banks.

Eleanor Roosevelt appeared on her first radio broadcast shortly after the election of her husband. The first broadcast from Vatican City was made on April 1,

Harry Frankel was famous as "Singing Sam, the Barbasol Man" and his deep bass voice introduced one of radio's first singing commercials. The words:

> Barbasol, Barbasol!
> No brush, no lather, no rub-in,
> Wet your face and then begin.
> Barbasol, Barbasol. . . .

Julia Sanderson and Frank Crummit may have been the first husband and wife team to reach radio stardom. They first appeared in 1929 on CBS for Blackstone Cigars and maintained their popularity for more than a decade. In the 1940's they presided over a quiz show called "The Battle of the Sexes."

during which the world listened to the ceremonies incident to Pope Pius' opening the Holy Door of the Basilica of St. Peter's.

On April 11, George Bernard Shaw was heard on NBC in one of his very first broadcasts, and in June comedian Bob Hope made his radio debut.

One of the important developments during the radio network's first decade of operation was the growth of radio's use as a means of direct contact between the people of the United States and their government. During his first nine months in office in 1932, President Roosevelt was heard on radio twenty times.

The country was listening to "Singing Sam, the Barbasol Man," to Frank Crummit and Julia Sanderson. They were listening to the smooth voice of David Ross read poetry on the air. Goodman Ace and his wife, Jane, entertained the public with their "Easy Aces" program. Edwin C. Hill became famous with his "Human Side of the News." Stoopnagle and Budd were high in the country's favor, and millions of people listened to Arthur Tracy, the "Street Singer," while the country danced to Fred Waring's Pennsylvanians, Isham Jones, Paul Whiteman, and to Ben Bernie and "All the Lads." The tunes, "Carioca," "Easter Parade," "Who's Afraid of the Big Bad Wolf?" and "The Isle of Capri" were popular.

Announcer David Ross, who became known for his poetry reading, is shown here with Helen Morgan and Harry Richman.

The "National Barn Dance," a popular radio program, began its series in August and the first regularly scheduled program from Europe was radioed to the United States in October. That same month, the *Graf Zeppelin*, while flying over the Atlantic from South American points to Miami, broadcast the event to the American people.

On November 11, NBC made its first broadcast from Radio City. Leading radio executives spoke, including M. H. Aylesworth, David Sarnoff, Owen D. Young and General James G. Harbord. The radio audience was also entertained by such artists as Jane Cowl, Jessica Dragonette, the Revelers, Frank Munn, Virginia Rea, Walter Damrosch, John McCormack, Maria Jeritza, Rudy Vallee, Will Rogers, Amos 'n' Andy, Paul Whiteman, and the Schola Cantorum Choir. The next day, a 400-piece symphony orchestra, the largest ever assembled for radio, broadcast from Radio City under a series of famous conductors.

In December, the first sponsored series of operas was inaugurated by the American Telephone and

Goodman Ace and his wife Jane gave the country one of the most polished comedy programs on the air—"Easy Aces." Ace, who went on to become one of television's top writers, devised and performed in this "folks next door" show. This is what "Easy Aces" sounded like:

ACE: Oh, hello, Jane. Didn't hear you come in. What are you doing downtown this early in the day?

JANE: Dear, I just did the most terrible thing I've ever done in all the years we've been married and ten months.

ACE: Uh? What did you—

JANE: But first I also want you to know I feel terrible about it and I'm gonna cancel it.

ACE: Cancel wha—

JANE: And I also want you to know I didn't do it of my own violation. I was talked into it, by somebody I should have *known* better.

ACE: But what did you—

JANE: And you know me when somebody talks me into something. When I get the urge to do it, I'm completely uninhabited.

ACE: Uninhab—

JANE: But no sooner had I done it when I realized what a mistake it was.

ACE: What mistake?

JANE: And I realize now that I could never wear it with a clear conscience no matter how cold it gets.

ACE: Never wear—

JANE: So I'm gonna cancel the whole thing this minute. May I use your phone?

ACE: No. Wait a minute. What did you do? Do you mean to say you ordered that mink coat without even waiting to find out if my deal went through or not?

JANE: In other words, yes.

ACE: In other words—

JANE: But don't worry, dear. I'm gonna cancel it. I told him to go ahead with it, but there's still time to stop him. I may have to pay the initial cost.

ACE: The initial cost—

JANE: I told him to put my initials in the lining.

ACE: Oh, the initial cost.

JANE: But, there's still time to cancel the coat. And no sooner said the better.

ACE: Well, Jane, look. You don't have to cancel it. I just put over that deal I was telling you about. So now you can get the coat with a clear science.

JANE: Oh, no, too late. I already did it. I'm going to cancel it as a lesson to me. A wife must take the bitter with the better, I always say.

ACE: Yes, you do always say.

JANE: A person can't just run around half crocked buying every little trinket and junket that comes to her mind.

ACE: Mink coat—trinket—

JANE: Exactly. And I'm gonna teach me a lesson if it's the last thing I do.

ACE: But look, Jane, I put the deal over. I can afford it now.

JANE: No—no—this hurts me more than it does you, dear, but it has to be done. I'll call him up right now. [*Dials.*

ACE: Well, if that's the way you feel about it.

JANE: I'm sorry but it has to be this way. And maybe after this I'll remember to at least ask my husband before I buy a mink coat. I don't know how I came to do such a thing. If I keep doing things like this, I'll be kissing my happy home good-by.

Ultra-screwball comedy was the forte of the redoubtable Colonel Lemuel Q. Stoopnagle (on ladder) and his friend Budd.

For many years Saturday night meant the "National Barn Dance" to millions of listeners. In 1936 the trio of Verne, Lee and Mary were favorites on the "Barn Dance." From left to right in this picture are Leone Hassel (Lee), Verne Hassell, and Evelyn Wood (Mary).

Telegraph Company, and later that month, the first program from India was heard in the United States over NBC.

By 1932 hundreds of new performers had appeared on radio, many of them destined to long stardom and others to fleeting popularity. The top performers on the air in 1932 included "Amos 'n' Andy" (Charles Correll and Freeman Gosden). The popularity of this program has held through many years and its still being broadcast both on radio and television. Other popular shows included the Lucky Strike program, B. A. Rolfe's orchestra, the Chase and Sanborn program starring Eddie Cantor with his violinist, Rubinoff, and Rudy Vallee starring for Fleischmann's Yeast. The "Palmolive Hour" and "True Story" with Mary and Bob were among the top ten programs. The Blackstone Cigar show starred Frank Crummit and Julia Sanderson, while Billy Jones and Ernie Hare, formerly the "Happiness Boys," starred in the Interwoven Show. Singer Morton Downey thrilled the hearts of American women on the Camel program.

In 1933 the "top ten" included the Maxwell House "Show Boat." Ed Wynn had moved in with his Texaco "Fire Chief" program and Al Jolson and Jack Pearl

Rubinoff, with his "magic violin," won little praise from music critics, but he probably played a large role in awakening the American public to the beauties of serious music.

"Yowsah . . ." Ben Bernie, the "Old Maestro," and "All the Lads" offered relaxing comedy and music during the 1930's. His sign-off theme song was one of the most memorable in radio. Here is how it went:

Au revoir, pleasant dreams!
Think of us when requesting your themes.
Until next Tuesday when
Possibly you may all tune in again,
Keep the Old Maestro always in your schemes.
Yowsah, yowsah, yowsah. . . .

Au revoir, this is Ben Bernie, ladies and gentlemen,
    and all the lads
Wishing you a bit of pleasant dreams.
May good luck and happiness, success, good health
    attend your schemes.
And don't forget, should you ever send in your re-
    quest-a,
Why, we'll sure try to do our best-a.
Yowsah . . .
Au revoir, a fond cherrio, a bit of a tweet-tweet, God
    bless you . . .
And pleasant dreams!

were rising in popularity. "Myrt and Marge" had moved ahead. "Sherlock Holmes" and the "Sinclair Wiener Minstrels" were included in the country's regular listening habits. A new and popular performer in 1933 was Walter O'Keefe on the Lucky Strike program. Ben Bernie emerged on the Pabst Blue Ribbon show, and Burns and Allen were entertaining the country on the White Owl program.

The year 1932 had marked the start of one of broadcasting's most successful stars, Jack Benny, who had moved up into the top ten in 1933, to sixth place in 1934, and to the top in 1935. 1934 saw the premier of one of the first musical comedies composed specifically for broadcasting, "The Gibson Family." The "Kraft Music Hall" began its long run on NBC, and Joe Penner was amusing the American radio public with his catch-phrases, "Wanna buy a duck?" and "You *nasty* man!" 1934 also saw the emergence of Harriet Hilliard and Ozzie Nelson on the Baker's broadcast, and in this year too Fred Allen became one of the leaders of radio entertainment.

The Federal Communications Commission began to

"Wanna buy a duck?" With the help of a few catch-phrases like that, which swept the country, Joe Penner became one of the top comics in radio.

Benny arriving in New York with Mary Livingstone and his on-the-air valet "Rochester" (Eddie Anderson). Figure in center is unidentified.

Jack Benny, one of radio's best-loved comedians, came to the medium in 1932. When he made his first guest appearance on Ed Sullivan's CBS program in March of that year, he introduced himself to the radio audience by saying, "Hello folks, this is Jack Benny. There will be a slight pause for everyone to say, 'Who cares?' "

Benny had entered vaudeville at 17, and later, as an enlistee in the Navy, appeared in the "Great Lakes Naval Revue." Out of the Navy, he became a violinist and did monologues, gradually building up the characterization of himself as the "stingiest man in the world." It was to be his radio trademark.

Benny's relaxed humor, depending almost entirely on situation and character rather than wisecracks, earned his Sunday night show number one rating for many years. One of the classic Jack Benny skits of all time involved a holdup man who demanded of Jack, "Your money or your life." The radio audience was treated to one of the longest silences ever aired. Finally, the holdup man yelled, "Well?" And Benny petulantly replied, "I'm thinking it over."

Benny's vintage Maxwell was one of the great running gags of radio, in a class with Fibber McGee's closet or Gracie Allen's lost brother.

The blunt tones of Al Smith, as Governor of New York and candidate for President in 1928, were familiar to millions of listeners. His pronunciation of "raddio" was famous. This 1934 picture shows Smith, in his famous brown derby, with Frances Perkins, Ann Morgan (behind the mike), and announcer Bob Trout.

Belle Baker, already famous as a singer and comedienne on the vaudeville stage, became a radio star via the Everready Blades "Radio Gaities" show in the early 1930's.

Frank Munn was a popular singer of classical and semiclassical music, appearing on such programs as the "American Album of Familiar Music."

Irene Wicker, the "Singing Lady," was a figure beloved by both children and their parents. She is shown above with her accompanist, Milton Rettenberg.

"Whispering Jack" Smith was a popular singer in the early 1930's. His soft, crooning style gave him his name.

George Gershwin made guest appearances on radio from time to time in the early 1930's.

"All right, all right!" Major Edward Bowes' "Amateur Hour" was one of the big shows of the 1930's. Everyone was familiar with his clanging gong, which signalled that a performer had struck out, and with his droned allusion to the wheel of fortune, "Round and round she goes, and where she stops nobody knows!" Many now-famous

names were introduced to the public on the "Amateur Hour" and the travelling "Major Bowes units," made up of winners on the program, provided employment for many entertainers during the depression.

Major Bowes, who built the Capitol Theatre in New York and at one time was vice-president of Goldwyn Films, started in radio with Roxy and His Gang and continued that series as "The Capitol Theater Family."

Strange musical aggregations, musical sawyers, impersonators, tap dancers, and whatnot flourished on the "Amateur Hour."

function on July 11, 1934, and was composed of seven commissioners appointed by the President and subject to the confirmation of the Senate. The FCC assumed the responsibility for American broadcasting and began to regulate the activities of radio and television.

The Mutual Broadcasting System came into being this year, when four stations, WGH, Chicago, WLW, Cincinnati, WXYZ, Detroit, and WOR, New York, agreed to organize for the purpose of soliciting more advertising for the stations. The new network promoted sales and set up land line connections for Mutual programming.

On July 26, 1934, Colonel Walter Adam broadcast the story of the murder of Chancellor Dollfuss from Vienna. In 1935, Haile Selassie, Emperor of Ethiopia, broadcast to the United States, pleading for help against the invading Italians. Radio had become a potent force in the world.

From March to December of 1935, Jack Benny had come into first place of the top ten. In third place, during this period, a new show emerged. It was Major Bowes' "Amateur Hour," broadcast for Chase and San-

Tenor Nino Martini and conductor Erno Rapee on the "Linit Seven-Star Revue" in 1933.

Jim and Marian Jordan ("Fibber McGee and Molly") broke into radio in 1925. They auditioned on station WJBO in Chicago and were immediately signed for a sponsored local show. Before radio they did a vaudeville act all over the country. In 1931, with Don Quinn, they created a series called "Smackout," which consisted of comedy and tall tales. The characters of "Fibber McGee and Molly" were introduced on this show and sky-rocketed to popularity. "Fibber McGee and Molly" kept their hold on the nation's affections through three decades, and in 1959 could still be heard on NBC's "Monitor."

Some samples of their humor:

FIBBER: Where's my order blank, Molly?
MOLLY: In your hand.
FIBBER: Oh, yes. Pencil, pencil, where's my pencil?

MOLLY: Behind your ear.
FIBBER: Which ear? Come, come, this is my very busy day. Which ear?
MOLLY: Your left ear, and don't get "executive" with me, dearie. I knew you when you thought a dotted line was a leopard.

MOLLY: I never knew whether you took up the mandolin because you loved music or hated paddling.
FIBBER: Remember the time you dropped my paddle out of the canoe applauding one of my songs and we had to paddle home with the mandolin?
MOLLY: I wasn't applauding, I was swatting a mosquito.
FIBBER: Wonder what's the best thing to polish it up with.
MOLLY: If you don't know that, dearie, you'd better learn to play that thing or take a course in scissors grinding.

Ed East and Ralph Dumke, the "Sisters of the Skillet," were a popular comedy team of the mid-1930's.

born Coffee. Major Bowes, his well-remembered gong and his "All right, all right!" were destined to take first place soon after and to stay at the top of the popularity poll until 1937. Another star in 1935 was Bing Crosby, who went on the air for Woodbury and almost immediately reached the top ten.

"Fibber McGee and Molly" began their very popular radio series in April, 1935. During this month, the first broadcast was made from the Coliseum in Rome on Easter Sunday, and Marconi's 61st birthday was saluted by the world. The Silver Jubilee celebration of King George V and Queen Mary was broadcast from St. Paul's Cathedral in London, and the Dionne Quintuplets celebrated their first birthday, with Dr. Dafoe and Canadian officials speaking to the radio audience. The Quints themselves were heard gurgling throughout the world. The *Normandie's* arrival in New York on her maiden voyage was broadcast, and the "Amer-

David Sarnoff, left, and Guglielmo Marconi, when they visited the RCA Communications Transmitting Center at Rocky Point, Long Island, in 1933.

Torch-singer Helen Morgan sings on a 1933 broadcast. The other figures are, left to right, Jacques Renard, a popular bandleader of the day; Henry Hayward, producer of the show; and actor-singer-composer Harry Richman.

Russ Columbo, a crooner who ranked with Crosby and Vallee before his untimely death in 1934, was killed when an antique gun he was cleaning suddenly went off. One of Columbo's great numbers was "Prisoner of Love."

Phil Baker was master of ceremonies on "Take It or Leave It," the quiz shows that put the expression "the sixty-four dollar question" into the language.

The "Columbia Workshop" was probably radio's finest dramatic program. Presented unsponsored by CBS, it broadcast plays, many of them highly experimental, written for radio by such writers as Archibald MacLeish, Norman Corwin, and Arch Oboler. This 1938 photo shows a rehearsal of "Air Raid" by Archibald MacLeish. From left to right are Orson Welles, Betty Garde, Ray Collins, William N. Robeson, director, and Mr. MacLeish.

Agnes Moorehead, one of radio's most accomplished actresses, appeared frequently on the "Columbia Workshop" and on Orson Welles' "Mercury Theatre on the Air." A personal triumph for her was her broadcast of the chilling "Sorry, Wrong Number."

ican Town Meeting of the Air" began on March 30.

This same year dramatic programs became popular. Programs like "Lux Radio Theatre," presented such brilliant performers as Helen Hayes. In 1936, radio comedy was more popular than ever. Such personalities as Phil Baker, Jack Oakie and Ed Wynn had regular and popular programs. This was the year that Eddie Cantor first debated with a character of appalling denseness called "Parkyakarkas." Burns and Allen were delighting radio listeners, and "Professor Quiz" introduced America to a new kind of program, the quiz show, in which he asked questions and gave prizes for the correct answer. CBS launched its famous "Columbia Workshop" in 1936.

The birth of the give-away and quiz programs took place somewhere in the mid-1930's. "Professor Quiz" became network CBS property during this period and inaugurated a question and answer technique providing silver dollars for correct answers. The first question Professor Quiz asked on his first program was, "What is the difference between a 'lama' with one 'l' and a 'llama' with two 'l's'?"

In 1936 the "Lux Radio Theatre," featuring Cecil

Helen Hayes

Tyrone Power

Barbara Stanwyck

*"Lux presents Holly-wood . . ."* Most of the brightest stars of stage and screen appeared at one time or another on the *"Lux Radio Theatre,"* with its distinguished host, Cecil B. DeMille. *(Above)* Janet Gaynor and Charles Farrell.

On December 12, 1936, a listening world heard the deep voice of Sir John Reith, Director of the British Broadcasting Corporation, say: "This is Windsor Castle. His Royal Highness, Prince Edward." And then came the tired voice of the man who only the day before had been King Edward VIII. This is what he said (in part):

"At long last I am able to say a few words of my own.

"I have never wanted to withhold anything, but until now it has not been constitutionally possible for me to speak.

"A few hours ago I discharged my last duty as King and Emperor, and now that I have been succeeded by my brother, the Duke of York, my first words must be to declare my allegiance to him. This I do with all my heart.

"You all know the reasons which have impelled me to renounce the Throne, but I want you to understand that in making up my mind I did not forget the Country or the Empire which, as Prince of Wales and lately as King, I have for 25 years tried to serve.

"But you must believe me when I tell you that I have found it impossible to carry the heavy burden of responsibility and to discharge my duties as King, as I would wish to do, without the help and support of the woman I love. . .

\* \* \*

"And now we all have a new King.

"I wish him, and you, his people, happiness and prosperity with all my heart.

"God bless you all.

"God save the King."

B. de Mille moved to sixth place in popularity. During this year, news of the death of King George V of England was broadcast around the world. In April, NBC made successful use of the micro-wave transmitter, so small that it could be concealed in George Hicks' silk top hat at a broadcast describing the annual Easter parade on New York's Fifth Avenue.

1936 was an election year and the networks provided the most exhaustive coverage to date of a Presidential race, which that year pitted Franklin D. Roosevelt against Republican Alfred M. Landon of Kansas.

On December 12, with the whole world listening, the man who had charmed the world as Prince of Wales announced his abdication of the throne he had held for only eleven months as King Edward VIII. He was doing so, he said, in order to marry "the woman I love," who, his listeners all knew, was Mrs. Wallis Warfield Simpson, an American and a divorcee. It was a brief but deeply human message, and the weary voice of the ex-King, magically wafted around the globe by radio, stirred hearts everywhere.

The first radio pick-up from Nanking, China, was made by NBC on December 17, as the headlines of the day focused on the kidnapping of General Chiang Kai-shek, in the seemingly endless struggle between China and Japan.

World news was being made in 1936 and 1937, and listeners were hearing dramatic radio accounts of the events. A full-scale civil war had broken out in Spain; German troops marched into the Rhineland; a French Socialist Government formed under Léon Blum; the

*"No names, please!"* John J. Anthony was the oracle of "The Good Will Hour," passing out advice on every conceivable human difficulty.

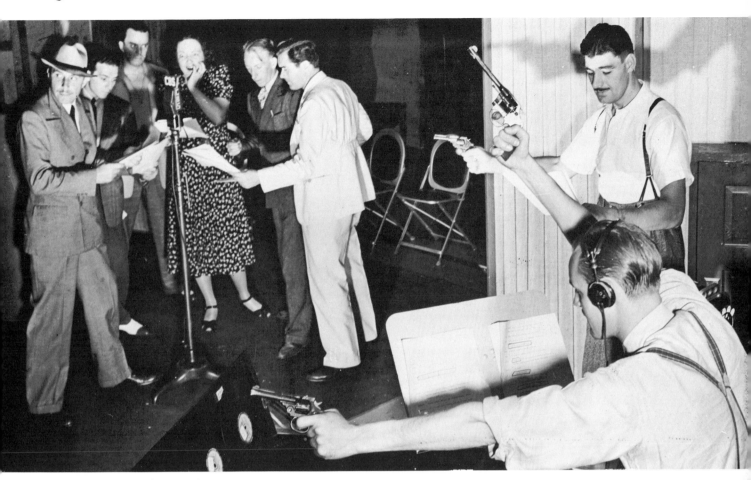

(*Rat-tat-tat of machine gun*)
(*Police sirens*)
(*Rat-tat-tat of machine guns*)
(*Shuffle of prisoners in prison yard*)
ANNOUNCER: "Gang Busters!"

This program achieved great popularity in the 1930's. Featuring true stories of crime and punishment, it was notable for its superb use of sound effects. In this 1936 picture a group of actors is clustered around the microphone in a tense scene while sound technicians provide the fireworks.

Missouri-born Mary Margaret McBride is considered the best known and most successful of all the conductors of women's broadcasts. *Printer's Ink*, the advertising trade magazine, once described her influence over her listeners as "perhaps the most outstanding reliance upon the word of a human being in the commercial field." What made her successful, probably, is her spontaneity and naturalness and her knack for being the perfect proxy for her listeners. When she interviews her guests, she asks the questions her audience would ask, and her reactions to the answers are theirs.

When Mary Margaret, as her millions of listeners called her, celebrated her tenth anniversary on the air, 20,000 people packed Madison Square Garden to do homage to her. A later Anniversary celebration filled Yankee Stadium.

W. C. Fields' frequent appearances on the "Chase and Sanborn Hour" were always memorable for his exchanges of vituperation with dummy Charlie McCarthy. Although this was supposed to be one of radio's familiar "feuds," friends of Fields claim that his dislike for the dummy was very genuine. Here are Fields, McCarthy and Edgar Bergen. Dorothy Lamour stands between the adversaries.

*"Bah, humbug!"* Although Lionel Barrymore appeared frequently on radio, and even had a series of his own called "Mayor of the Town," it is for his yearly portrayal of Ebenezer Scrooge in Dickens' "A Christmas Carol" that he is most fondly remembered.

Although his clipped accents had been heard on radio since 1928, H. V. Kaltenborn reached the peak of his fame during the Munich crisis of 1938. He didn't leave the CBS studios for the whole period of its duration, and went on the air 85 times to analyze the news that was pouring in from Europe. For the first time in radio's history a news program attracted larger audiences than entertainment shows, and radio's position as the nation's prime source of news and interpretation was firmly established. *(Above)* Kaltenborn in about 1929; *(below)* Kaltenborn in 1938.

Some NBC stars of the late 1930's. From left to right, Bob Burns with his "bazooka"; Tommy Riggs, who exchanged banter with a fictitious little girl named Betty Lou; Charlie McCarthy; Edgar Bergen; Rudy Vallee; and Joe Penner with his famous duck.

Rome-Berlin Axis was created, an alliance that was destined to shake the world and to destroy millions of innocent people.

John Barrymore appeared in a series of six of Shakespeare's plays in 1937. CBS moved its television transmitters to the top of the Chrysler Building and established a full-scale studio plant in nearby Grand Central Terminal.

Don Ameche, an old radio hand, having appeared in soap operas at one time and starred on "The First Nighter," reached the top in 1937, when he took over M.C. duties on "The Chase and Sanborn Hour"—a job that included enduring the insults of rambunctious Charlie McCarthy.

One of radio's best-remembered personalities, Bob Burns, joined Bing Crosby's "Kraft Music Hall" that year. Burns, with his tales of "Granpaw Snazzy" and other members of his Van Buren, Arkansas, family, was a genuine folk humorist. His famous "bazooka," a Rube Goldberg-ish musical instrument, became so much a part of the nation's vocabulary that the name was given to a U.S. Army rocket launcher during World War II.

On May 6, 1937, Herbert Morrison of WLS, Chicago, was on hand at Lakehurst, New Jersey, to describe the arrival of the German dirigible *Hindenburg* to the radio audience. What happened, of course, is history. The enormous airship exploded and burned, and Morrison, almost in tears, gave his listeners one of the most hair-raising eyewitness reports ever broadcast.

An event that illustrates the importance of radio in

Shakespeare came to the networks in the summer of 1937, when both CBS and NBC presented cycles of his plays with star-studded casts. The leading players in the CBS "Hamlet" were Montague Love (upper left) as the King, Burgess Meredith (upper right) in the title role, Walter Abel (lower left) as Horatio, and Grace George as the Queen. Other plays starred such actors as Thomas Mitchell, Edward G. Robinson and Rosalind Russell. NBC presented the great John Barrymore.

Milton Berle entered the entertainment field when he was five years old, at the old Biograph studios in Fort Lee, New York. He made his film debut as the baby Marie Dressler clutched to her heart in *Tillie's Punctured Romance.* Born in 1908, Berle played his first stage role in 1920 and later toured the country in a vaudeville act. He did his first comedy work in 1926, and in 1931 made a tremendous hit in a solo act at the Palace Theatre in New York. Engagements in night clubs and theaters all over the country followed. Berle later returned to Broadway in shows produced by Earl Carroll and Florenz Ziegfeld. He did numerous radio shows throughout the 1930's and 1940's, but his biggest success was to come in television. *(Right)* With the Murphy Sisters in 1946.

the nation's life took place on the evening of December 12, 1937. Mae West made a guest appearance on the "Chase and Sanborn Hour" that night, and the sexy inflections in her voice during her repartee with dummy Charlie McCarthy set off a storm of protest from the public that led eventually to an FCC investigation. Reviewing the case in its October 15, 1956, issue, *Broadcasting and Telecasting* Magazine said:

In essence, Miss West and Charlie kicked around a "come up and see me sometime" dialogue. If the script looked reasonably innocent, the way the two read their lines left a lot of listeners convinced they were hearing night clubbish entertainment instead of the more careful comedy of the air lanes. Miss West reeked of seduction. The resulting

Fiorello H. La Guardia, Mayor of New York from 1934 to 1945, took his program for reforms and improvements directly to the people via radio. During a newspaper strike in 1937 he read the comic strips to the kids and reported the news to their parents.

In the 1935-36 season Frances Langford starred on "Hollywood Hotel," an hour-long weekly variety show with Dick Powell as master of ceremonies. The program featured a twenty-minute dramatic production with Hollywood stars, introduced by gossip columnist Louella Parsons.

Kay Kyser, a popular band leader, delighted audiences with his "Kollege of Musical Knowledge," a program which combined elements of the quiz show and the musical variety show. When a contestant did not know the answer to a question, "Professor" Kyser's call of "Students!" would bring the answer from the studio audience.

Leslie Howard, here shown with his daughter Leslie Ruth in 1936, was a frequent performer on radio dramatic shows.

Phil Cook was a popular CBS performer in the mid-1930's. He played the guitar, sang, and chatted with the radio audience.

"*Time . . . marches on!*" A phenomenally successful news broadcast was "The March of Time," in which the leading events of the week were dramatized. The identity of the famous "March of Time" voice was kept secret for years and later revealed as that of Westbrook Van Voorhis. In the scene pictured here are actors Ted de Corsie, Bill Adams, and Paul Stewart in 1938.

Ted Husing interviews Joe Louis after the famous Louis-Sharkey fight of 1936.

routine was more devastating than the program producers had anticipated, and the post-broadcast results astonished all concerned. Demands for a Congressional probe were made on Capitol Hill and religious interests voiced indignation. Newspapers had a field day with colorful stories and stern editorials.

"Big Town" with Edward G. Robinson heading a large cast moved into the top ten in 1938. Kay Kyser and his "Kollege of Musical Knowledge" made their radio debut in March, and the first NBC television showing of scenes from a Broadway show, *Susan and God*, starring Gertrude Lawrence, was presented on June 7.

The Joe Louis-Max Schmeling fight was given the

Speaking with a kind of breathless intensity, Clem McCarthy became famous as a sports announcer. He is shown here describing the Louis-Schmeling fight in 1938. For millions McCarthy's gravelly voice sounding "They're off!" was an inseparable part of horse racing.

NEW YORK, MONDAY, OCTOBER 31, 1938.

# Radio Listeners in Panic, Taking War Drama as Fact

## Many Flee Homes to Escape 'Gas Raid From Mars'—Phone Calls Swamp Police at Broadcast of Wells Fantasy

A wave of mass hysteria seized thousands of radio listeners throughout the nation between 8:15 and 9:30 o'clock last night when a broadcast of a dramatization of H. G. Wells's fantasy, "The War of the Worlds," led thousands to believe that an interplanetary conflict had started with invading Martians spreading wide death and destruction in New Jersey and New York.

The broadcast, which disrupted households, interrupted religious services, created traffic jams and clogged communications systems, was made by Orson Welles, who as the radio character, "The Shadow," used to give "the creeps" to countless child listeners. This time at least a score of adults required medical treatment for shock and hysteria.

In Newark, in a single block at Heddon Terrace and Hawthorne Avenue, more than twenty families rushed out of their houses with wet handkerchiefs and towels over their faces to flee from what they believed was to be a gas raid. Some began moving household furniture.

Throughout New York families left their homes, some to flee to near-by parks. Thousands of persons called the police, newspapers and radio stations here and in other cities of the United States and Canada seeking advice on protective measures against the raids.

The program was produced by Mr. Welles and the Mercury Theatre on the Air over station WABC and the Columbia Broadcasting System's coast-to-coast network, from 8 to 9 o'clock.

The radio play, as presented, was to simulate a regular radio program with a "break-in" for the material of the play. The radio listeners, apparently, missed or did not listen to the introduction, which was: "The Columbia Broadcasting System and its affiliated stations present Orson Welles and the Mercury Theatre on the Air in 'The War of the Worlds' by H. G. Wells."

They also failed to associate the program with the newspaper listing of the program, announced as "Today: 8:00-9:00—Play: H. G. Wells's 'War of the Worlds'—WABC." They ignored three additional announcements made during the broadcast emphasizing its fictional nature

Mr. Welles opened the program with a description of the series of

**Continued on Page Four**

ANNOUNCER: From the Meridian Room of the Park Plaza in New York City, we bring you the music of Ramon Raquello and his Orchestra. With a touch of the Spanish, Ramon leads off with "La Cumparsita." (Music starts)

ANNOUNCER 2: Ladies and Gentlemen, we interrupt our program of dance music to bring you a special bulletin. At 20 minutes before 8 o'clock Central Time, Professor Farrell of Mt. Jennings Observatory, Chicago, reports observing several explosions of incandescent gas occurring at regular intervals on the planet Mars.

After this came more dance music, and further bulletins about disturbances on Mars. Then came a flash with the shocking news that a giant meteor had landed near Princeton, New Jersey, killing 1500 people. Dance music again, and then the appalling bulletin that it had not been a meteor but a huge metal cylinder containing Martians armed with death rays. There were on-the-spot reports and interviews with scientists. An official-sounding voice pleaded with the nation to remain calm.

But the nation wasn't remaining calm. By this time even people who had been with the program from the beginning were no longer sure if what they were hearing was fact or fiction. Panic was mounting all over the country. Two professors from the Princeton geology department, who hadn't waited to hear the more alarming bulletins, had set out to locate the "meteors." In one block in Newark more than twenty families rushed out of their homes with wet handkerchiefs over their faces to protect themselves from "gas." A woman in Pittsburgh was stopped as she prepared to take poison, saying, "I'd rather die this way than that." A high school girl in Pennsylvania interviewed later said, "I was really hysterical. My two girl friends and I were crying and holding each other, and everything seemed so unimportant in the face of death."

Before the program was over, CBS, its switchboards swamped with frantic calls, began to make special announcements to the effect that it was only a play, but the damage had been done, and the announcements had to continue all evening before the nation would quiet down.

Between 8 and 9 o'clock (EST) on the night of October 30, 1938, the lion's share of the radio audience, if the rating services could be trusted, should have been laughing at Charlie McCarthy on the "Chase and Sanborn Hour." But maybe there was something wrong with the ratings, because that night another program on another network at the same time almost succeeded in scaring the nation out of its wits.

This was Orson Welles' famous "Hallowe'en spoof."

"The Columbia Broadcasting System and its affiliated stations," intoned the announcer as usual at the beginning, "present Orson Welles and the Mercury Theatre of the Air in *The War of the Worlds* by H. G. Wells." But, oddly, what followed was a weather report, and then:

In 1938 Orson Welles, at 23, was a stage and radio veteran of fabled versatility. The Mercury Theatre, which he helped found, came to radio fresh from its 1937 triumphs on Broadway in Welles' modern-dress version of *Julius Caesar*. The company included such fine actors as Ray Collins, Everett Sloane, and Joseph Cotten. Not too well known is the fact that Welles at one time was the voice of "The Shadow" in the radio mystery series of the same name.

He is shown here being interviewed by reporters after the "Martian" broadcast.

most extensive coverage of any sporting event in radio history. It was carried to every section of the world except the Orient. Five separate sets of announcers at the ring side gave descriptions in English, Spanish, Portuguese and German. Clem McCarthy and Ed Thorgersen reported for the United States.

In 1938, the radio audience heard "a world in turmoil" on CBS "World News Roundup." Many voices became well known—Shirer from London, Mowror from Paris, Huss from Berlin, Ed Murrow from Vienna, and Bob Trout from Washington.

Any doubt of radio's impact was dispelled on October 30, 1938, when Orson Welles, then a precocious dramatist-actor of 23, presented as a Hallowe'en prank a fantasy about an invasion from Mars, which brought cold terror to several millions of America and very nearly set off a nation-wide panic.

The FCC and the Columbia Broadcasting System received hundreds of complaints about the incident, and after considering the problem, the Federal authority advised broadcasters strongly to avoid any repetition of this incident. Simulated news broadcasts were to be avoided at all costs. The network was profuse in its apologies, but it pointed out, justly, that the

Raymond Gram Swing was one of the new breed of serious news analysts who helped a confused American public understand the fast-moving events in Europe.

The incomparable (as she was billed) Hildegarde preparing for a 1939 appearance on "Raymond Paige, 99 Men, and a Girl." With her is Mr. Paige. Hildegarde really hit her stride in radio during the war years, when she had her own weekly show.

Dinah Shore became popular in the late 1930's, when she could be heard singing with the "Chamber Music Society of Lower Basin Street" and on the Eddie Cantor show. She was one of Cantor's many successful protégés.

program was announced as a play at the beginning and interrupted three times for similar announcements.

Both houses of Congress this same year established radio galleries, providing facilities for radio commentators. A series of 34 radio broadcasts in connection with the visit of King George VI and Queen Elizabeth to America was made.

1939 was a year of fast-moving, earth-shaking events. Hitler had demanded that Germany must have Danzig. Prime Minister Chamberlain explained England's position in a radio broadcast, and on September 3, England's Declaration of War on Germany was broadcast to the world. The same day Premier Daladier of France broadcast his country's Declaration of War on Germany. World War II had officially begun.

In 1939, another group of long-time radio favorites made its way into the top ten. Fourth place was taken by "Fibber McGee and Molly," Kate Smith reached the top ten that year, and Bob Hope joked his way into seventh place. Number one and two were the "Chase and Sanborn Hour" and Jack Benny. In 1940, "The Aldrich Family" made a spectacular rise from fortieth to sixth place. Another new name on the roster was that of Kay Kyser.

The period of great development was coming to an end. Three major factors had played their roles in the brief history of radio advertising, network operation, and government regulation. While there was little change in numbers of stations during this decade, radio's importance in the American scene had nonetheless grown enormously.

"Myrt and Marge," in 1931, with Myrtle Vail as Myrt, Ray Hedge as Clarence Tiffingtuffer, Dora Damerel as Marge, and Jeanne Juvalier as Mrs. Armstrong.

Probably no other form of radio entertainment has been more popular, more scorned, and more enduring than the daytime serial, usually inelegantly tagged the "soap opera." Several of those still to be heard on the networks today are hugging the quarter-century mark, their characters not a whit aged despite the almost unbelievable vicissitudes they have weathered. "Helen Trent," for example, past thirty-five when the serial went on the air in 1933 and by any mundane reckoning now in her mid-sixties, in 1960 was still recapturing romance daily.

What, exactly, is a soap opera?

"A soap opera," wrote James Thurber in his *New Yorker*

Virginia Payne, Murray Forbes, and Charles Egelston in "Ma Perkins."

series called "Soapland," "is a kind of sandwich, whose recipe is simple enough, although it took years to compound. Between thick slices of advertising spread twelve minutes of dialogue, add predicament, villainy, and female suffering in equal measure, throw in a dash of nobility, sprinkle with tears, season with organ music, cover with a rich announcer sauce, and serve five times a week."

The origins of this toothsome sandwich are obscure, but it seems fairly certain that the form began in Chicago in the late 1920's and was probably inspired by the success of "Amos 'n' Andy." But Marian and Jim Jordan ("Fibber McGee and Molly") lay legitimate claim to having created a forerunner of the soap opera in their "The Smith Family," heard in 1925. By 1932, at any rate, the daytime serial was in full flower. Elaine Carrington's "Red Davis"—later to become "Pepper Young's Family"—was on the air that year, and "Just Plain Bill," the creation of Charles D.

Andrews, was already neglecting his barber shop to assist his neighbors in their abundant adversities.

Between the two of them, Mrs. Carrington and Mr. Andrews (who was employed by Frank Hummert, the Sol Hurok of soap opera) turned out a prodigiously large proportion of the serials that saturated the daytime airwaves over twenty-five years. Besides "Pepper Young's Family" Mrs. Carrington created "When a Girl Marries," "Marriage for Two," and "Rosemary." Andrews was also responsible for "Backstage Wife" and "Ma Perkins," a show once described by *Variety* as " 'Just Plain Bill' in skirts." Another prolific writer is Irma Philips, who created "Road of Life," "The Right to Happiness," and "The Guiding Light."

Although the soap operas have been ridiculed for their stereotyped characters and plots, their humorlessness, their incredible elongation of time (which makes it easy for the

"One Man's Family." Minetta Ellen (extreme left) played Fanny and J. Anthony Smythe (extreme right) played Father Barbour through the 27-year run of this classic.

housewife to follow the plot even though she hears only one or two instalments a week) and for the mysterious ills to which Soapland's denizens succumb with monotonous regularity, the fact remains that the best of them have been very good indeed. Gertrude Berg's "The Goldbergs," for example, depicted well-delineated characters with warmth and humor, as did Paul Rhymer's "Vic and Sade." Of the latter program Edgar Lee Masters is said to have remarked that it presented the best American humor of its day. George Foster Peabody awards for radio excellence have gone to Sandra Michael's "Against the Storm" and to Carleton E. Morse's "One Man's Family," a venerable

nighttime series joined the daytime ranks in 1958 and finally expired in 1959.

Good or bad, the soap operas have had an enormous following. Millions of listeners take the anguished lives of their favorite characters very much to heart, writing them letters of advice and encouragement and even sending them gifts when births, weddings or other happy occasions in the story warrant them.

Many soap opera classics have disappeared in recent years, among them such hardies as "Stella Dallas," "Young Widder Brown," "Life Can Be Beautiful" ("Elsie Beebe," to the profession), and "Our Gal Sunday." But early in the

Vic and Sade, with their son Rush.

year 1960 it was still possible to tune in every weekday afternoon and hear, among others, "The Woman in My House," "Pepper Young's Family," "The Romance of Helen Trent," "Ma Perkins," "Young Doctor Malone," and "The Right to Happiness."

Julie Stevens and David Gothard in "The Romance of Helen Trent."

*Part Four:* THE FORTIES

WGAN-Saturday Night Serenade
WGY-Dinner Dance
WHAM-Hank & Herb
WHDH-Alec Templeton Time;
  Musical Concert
WJAR-Supper Show
WMCA-Sports
WMEX-Popular Music
WNAC-Musical Roundup
WNBC-Pappy Howard's Wagon
  Trail

Karnac. WOL WELI WNBC
WTRY CFCF WORC
CBS-Report to the Nation:
  WABC WOKO WGAN WTAG
  WABI WDRC WEEI WBRY
  WPRO WLAW
MBS-American Eagle Club:
  WATR WNBH WNLC WSAR
  WEAN WNAC
NBC-The Day of Reckoning:
  WEAF WTIC WCSH WFEA
  WJAR WLBZ WHAM WGY
  WBZ

CBC-Songs at Eventide: CBL
  CBO CHSJ CBA CFNB CBM
  CBF
CFCF-Studio Prgm.
WCSH-To be announced
WHAM-Lone Ranger
WHN-Adrienne Ames
WJAR-Eyes & Ears of the Air
  Force
★WMCA-News
WMEX-Vocal Spotlight
WNBH-Singing Troubador

Front
WHN-Word of Life Hour
WLAW-Advent Christian Church
★WMCA-News; Dance Party
WMEX-Musicale
WNEW-The Magic of Music
WOKO-Eyes & Ears of Air Force
WORC-Masterworks of Music
WQXR-Symphony Hall
WSAR-Dance Music
WTHT-Musiel Polish Prgm.

**8:15 P.M.**

BN-Boston Symphony Orchestra;
  Serge Koussevitzky, cond.:
  WJZ CBF WMFF WTRY CFCF
  WNBC WELI WORC WHDH
  On April 3, while the Boston
  Symphony Orchestra is on tour,
  a Gilbert and Sullivan operetta,
  starring Wilbur Evans, baritone,
  will be heard at this time.
WGAN-Dance Jamboree
WHAM-American Destiny
WMEX-Popular Music
WNEW-Popular Music
WOKO-Lest We Forget
WSAR-The Latin Quarter

**8:30 P.M.**

★MBS-Upton Close, news: WATR
  WNBH WNLC WSAR WTHT
  WEAN WOR WNAC
★CBS-Hobby Lobby; Dave El-
  man, m.c.; Eric Sevareid,
  news: WABC WOKO WGAN
  WPRO WLAW WTAG
BN-Boston Symphony Orch.:
  WJZ WTRY CFCF WORC
NBC-Truth or Consequences;
  Ralph Edwards, m.c.: WEAF
  WTIC WCSH WTAG WHAM
  WGY WBZ WLBZ WFEA
CBC-Share the Wealth: CBA CBL
  CBO CBM CHSJ CFNB
★WABI-Waltz Time; News
WBRY-Lest We Forget
WCAX-Sports
WHN-Final Rewrite
★WMCA-News; Ralph Cooper
WMEX-Uncle Bill's Common
  Sense Advice
★WNEW-News

**8:45 P.M.**

MBS-To be announced: WATR
  WNBH WNLC WSAR WTHT
  WEAN WOR WNAC
★WABI-The Marines March; Eric
  Sevareid
★WBRY-Your Army Reporter;
  Eric Sevareid, news
★WCAX-Music; Eric Sevareid
★WHN-News

**9:00 P.M.**

NBC-Alka-Seltzer National Barn
  Dance; Joe Kelly; Eddie Pea-
  body; Pat Buttram; Hoosier
  Hot Shots; Lulu Belle &
  Scotty; Dinning Sisters: WEAF
  WTIC WGY WCSH WFEA
  WJAR WBZ WHAM WORC
  See sponsor's announcement on
  this page.
MBS-Chicago Theater of the Air;
  Marion Claire; Symph. Orch.:
  WATR WNBH WNLC WNAC
  WSAR WTHT WOR WEAN
★CBC-News; Hockey Game:
  CBA CBL CBO CBM CFNB
  CHSJ CBF
CBS-Your Hit Parade; Frank
  Sinatra; Ethel Smith; Martin
  Bloch; Joan Edwards; Mark
  Warnow's Orch.: WABC
  WOKO WCAX WABI WEEI
  WBRY WDRC WGAN WPRO
  WLAW WTAG
BN-Boston Symphony Orch.:
  WJZ WLBZ WTRY

---

# SATURDAY'S BEST LISTENING

*See program listings for more detail and additional news programs*

## News and Discussion

P.M.
4:00 Elmer Davis Comments on the
  War, MBS
5:45 Alex Dreier, NBC
6:15 People's Platform, CBS
  Lyman Bryson, moderator
7:00 Report to the Nation, CBS
8:00 Roy Porter, BN
8:30 Upton Close, MBS
9:15 Edward Tomlinson, BN
10:00 John B. Hughes, BN
10:00 News Analysis, BN
  April 3 and 17, John Gunther; April 10
  and 24, John W. Vandercook

## Variety

A.M.
9:00 Breakfast Club, BN
  Don McNeill, m.c.

P.M.
6:30 Hawaii Calls, MBS
7:30 Thanks to the Yanks, CBS
  Bob Hawk, m.c.
8:00 Frank Crumit and Julia Sanderson, CBS
8:30 Truth or Consequences, NBC
  Ralph Edwards, m.c.

8:30 Hobby Lobby, CBS
  Dave Elman, m.c.
9:00 Alka-Seltzer Nat'l Barn Dance,
  NBC
  Joe Kelly; Eddie Peabody; Pat Buttram;
  Hoosier Hot Shots; Lulu Belle & Scotty
9:00 Your Hit Parade, CBS
  Frank Sinatra; Joan Edwards; Ethel
  Smith; Mark Warnow's Orchestra
9:30 Victory Parade of Spotlight
  Bands, BN
10:00 Bill Stern's Colgate Sports News-
  reel, NBC
10:15 Bond Wagon, MBS
10:15 Campana Serenade, NBC
  Dick Powell; Music Maids; Matty Mal-
  neck's Orchestra
10:15 Blue Ribbon Town, CBS
  Groucho Marx; Virginia O'Brien; Donald
  Dickson; Robert Armbruster's Orchestra

## Drama

A.M.
11:30 Little Blue Playhouse, BN
P.M.
12:00 Theater of Today, CBS
12:30 Stars Over Hollywood, CBS
5:00 Doctors at War, NBC
7:00 The Strange Stories of Dr. Karnac, BN
7:00 The Day of Reckoning, NBC
7:30 Ellery Queen, NBC
8:00 Abie's Irish Rose, NBC
  Mercedes McCambridge; Richard Coogan;
  Alan Reed; Walter Kinsella

## Classical Music

P.M.
2:00 Metropolitan Opera, BN
  Three April broadcasts are scheduled for
  the Metropolitan Opera, April 3, 10 and 17
5:00 Cleveland Orchestra, CBS
  Arthur Rodzinski, conductor
8:15 Boston Symphony Orchestra,
  BN
  On April 3 a Gilbert and Sullivan operetta,
  starring Wilbur Evans, baritone, will be
  presented at this time
9:00 Chicago Theater of the Air, MBS
  Marion Claire; Symphony Orchestra
9:45 Saturday Night Serenade, CBS
  Jessica Dragonette, soprano; Bill Perry,
  tenor; The Serenaders; Gustave Haen-
  schen's Orchestra

Choice listening on a Saturday in 1943. (BN refers to Blue Network, now known as the American Broadcasting Company.)

"Wake up, America—time to stump the experts!" "Information Please" was perhaps the most urbane quiz program ever on radio. Regulars on the show were, left to right, Oscar Levant, John Kieran, Clifton Fadiman (moderator), and Franklin P. Adams. A different guest joined the panel every week.

# The Forties

By 1940 radio had become so big and so important in the United States that it frequently set the pattern for all other fields of entertainment. Radio stars were better known than most stage and screen stars, and frequently Hollywood paid huge sums to sign up radio personalities for pictures. Stars like Bing Crosby, Eddie Cantor, Joe Penner, Burns and Allen, Jack Benny, Kay Kyser, and the Andrews Sisters—people essentially identified with radio—were recruited to make movies in Hollywood. Often the films they appeared in had radio backgrounds, the *Big Broadcast* series, for example. It was a case of the tail of the dog growing so big and powerful that it was wagging the dog itself.

A new complication entered the radio scene in the mid-1940's—F.M. broadcasting. The letters stand for frequency modulation, a system of radio broadcasting and receiving that greatly improves the fidelity of sound and all but eliminates static.

The first United States patent on frequency modulation was issued in 1903, but it was not until 1933 that a practical application was found. Edwin Armstrong, an engineer with numerous other radio contributions to his credit, including the superheterodyne circuit,

had improved F.M. to the extent where it created both excitement and hostility in the radio industry. In 1934 and 1935 he conducted tests with the cooperation of RCA.

In 1936 the FCC became interested in the new medium and assigned the first experimental F.M. channel. Because the interests of F.M. conflicted with those of television, then in its infancy, only thirteen channels were assigned by 1939, the distribution of which were unfavorable to the medium.

In 1940 the FCC assigned F.M. to channels in the 42-50 megacycle band, but World War II caused a freeze in its further development.

In 1945 F.M. was assigned to the 88-108 megacycle bands, outmoding all sets built originally for the lower band. But now it seemed that F.M. was here to stay, and the major stations jumped on the bandwagon, taking out F.M. licenses. When, around 1948, television began its rapid expansion, the number of F.M. stations decreased. Those remaining became duplicates of the A.M. stations to which they belonged. It would not be until the "high fidelity" craze of the 1950's developed that F.M. would once more come into its own.

# Radio Reports World War II

"This . . . is . . . London." These were the dramatic words that started the daily broadcasts of Edward R. Murrow, London war correspondent of the Columbia Broadcasting System, and chief of its European staff. Mr. Murrow stirred the heart and conscience of America in his portrayal of the tension under which Londoners lived as they awaited the daily bombings of the Nazis' Luftwaffe.

Between bombings, Murrow planned radio coverage of the war as it progressed. He is shown here with Bill Henry, another CBS radio correspondent, who covered actual scenes of the bombings with iron hat and gas mask.

With World War II in full swing, networks were broadcasting to the country the fast-moving events that were changing the maps of the world. In May of 1940, Winston Churchill broadcast for the first time as England's Prime Minister. In June, radio audiences heard the German-French armistice proceedings from France.

This was the year that Selective Service started in the United States, and the country gathered around its radio to hear President Roosevelt draw the first draft number. German aircraft dropped hundreds of tons of heavy explosives and incendiaries on the City of London. America listened to an American voice, coming from a bomb shelter in England, start the day's broadcast with the portentous words, "This . . . is . . . London." It was the voice of Edward R. Murrow, a CBS war correspondent, bringing a dramatic account of events of war.

It was 2:30 P.M. in the East and 1:30 in the Middle West on December 7, 1941, when six million families who were listening to their radios, were told that the Japanese had attacked Pearl Harbor. It came as a sharp, peremptory shock as the newsrooms of all networks broke in on the Sunday afternoon programs with the bulletin: "The Japanese have attacked Pearl Harbor by air. President Roosevelt has just announced . . ."

Eric Sevareid (*above*) covered the war in the China-Burma-India Theatre, and Farnsworth Fowle (*below*) reported the victories in Italy and Sicily, both for CBS.

Winston M. Burdett (*above*) covered North Africa, and Howard K. Smith (*below*) covered Berlin before 1941 for CBS. Later, when the Nazis refused to let Smith make his broadcasts, he moved to Switzerland, and continued to report the war developments to the nation.

Larry Lesueur, one of CBS's war correspondents, covered an assignment on a British cargo ship which travelled through mine-infested waters from England to the coastline of the Soviet Union.

Charles Collingwood reported the North African campaign for CBS.

And on the following day, Franklin D. Roosevelt, broadcasting to a joint session of Congress and to the country, asked for a declaration of war against the Japanese. "Mr. Vice-President, Mr. Speaker, members of the Senate and the House of Representatives," said the President. "Yesterday, December 7, 1941, a date that will live in infamy, the United States of America was suddenly and deliberately attacked by naval and air forces of the Empire of Japan. . . . I ask Congress declare that since the unprovoked and dastardly attack by Japan on Sunday, December 7, 1941, a state of war has existed between the United States and the Japanese Empire."

Four days later, Germany and Italy were added to the roster of the enemy. Sixty million Americans had heard the historic broadcast.

In 1941, three new programs had moved up into the top ten. They were Lowell Thomas and the news, "Mr. District Attorney," and Red Skelton. Burns and Allen moved back into the picture, and four others, "Dr. Christian" (starring Jean Hersholt), Rudy Vallee, "Your Hit Parade," and "Big Town," dropped out of the leading group.

As the war progressed, networks gave increasing coverage to the events. This picture shows some NBC war correspondents at the scene of action. They are: Francis McCall, Wright Bryan, David Anderson, Tom Traynor (who was killed in action), and W. W. Chaplin.

As the fury of World War II mounted, increased coverage by all radio networks was provided. Analytical teamwork provided background for communiqués, exploded rumors and penetrated propaganda. Incisive appraisal of war developments was provided by Elmer Davis (*left*) and George Fielding Eliot.

George Fielding Eliot, the military analyst; Paul W. White, director of news broadcasts; and Quentin Reynolds, news analyst gave the radio audience an interpretation of the Allied invasion of Europe over CBS.

Charles Shaw (*above*) was a CBS correspondent in London, while Richard Curt Hottelet (*below*) covered Berlin before the United States entered the war.

This picture, taken somewhere in France, shows the exterior view of a press wireless truck, which was the first civilian radio station to link America and France with direct dispatches from Normandy after the invasion. It began regular service on June 13th directly from the beachhead. Messages were picked up at the press wireless receiving station at Baldwin, L.I., and relayed to the Times Square control headquarters and then distributed to the press.

One of the radio highspots of the second anniversary of World War II was the broadcast from London on CBS, during which many leaders of Nazi conquered countries resolved to bring about the liberation of their people. This radioed picture, taken in Columbia's London headquarters, shows: *(left to right)* Jan Masaryk, foreign minister of Czechoslovakia; Charalambos Simopoulos, Greek minister to London; King Haakon of Norway; Edward R. Murrow, CBS European bureau chief; Hubert Pierlot, Belgian premier; Anthony Biddle, American ambassador; Brendan Bracken, British minister of information; General Sikorski, Polish premier; Pieter Gerbrandy, premier of Holland; and Joseph Bech, Luxembourg foreign minister.

In his "Spirit of '41," John Daly, as a CBS news reporter, provided the country with news of important war developments.

In a 1942 series called "This Is War," Fredric March described to the American people the horrors and issues of the world-wide conflict.

"Vox Pop," an interview program, became especially popular during World War II, when it carried the voices of countless servicemen into their homes. Parks Johnson moderated the show.

It was the stirring broadcast of the electrocution of Bruno Hauptmann, Lindbergh kidnapper, in 1935 that propelled Gabriel Heatter from the rank of newsman to $3500-a-week commentator; but it was his "voice of doom" approach to the news during the war that established him as a top radio personality.

On June 22, 1941, listeners heard the news of the German invasion of Russia. American radio correspondents all over the world were sending back eyewitness accounts of war activities, and eventually they would accompany our troops as they stormed the beaches of Sicily and Normandy, and stand on the deck of the battleship "Missouri" as General MacArthur accepted the surrender of the Japanese. From far away places came the voices of Edward R. Murrow, William L. Shirer, Albert Warner, Bill Henry, and many others.

At home, the calm Hoosier twang of Elmer Davis inspired confidence, as he analyzed the day's news lucidly and honestly.

These were difficult times, but the country was still being entertained and charmed by radio personalities. Jack Benny on the "Jell-O" program was still in the top ten in 1941. "Fibber McGee and Molly," Edgar Bergen and Charlie McCarthy, Bob Hope and Ezra Stone (as "Henry Aldrich") were bringing their special types of entertainment into the American living rooms.

In 1940, the Republican and Democratic Conven- tions were televised, making pioneer use of the coaxial cable for long distance television relay purposes. The same year WNBT, New York and WRGB, Schenectady, were joined by radio relay for a re-broadcast test.

Meanwhile, the Milwaukee *Journal* had filed the first application to broadcast television programs on a commercial basis.

In 1942, Graham McNamee broadcast the story of the fire on the *Normandie* in New York Harbor. Eric Sevareid was broadcasting about Guadalcanal. During this period, radio audiences heard Mark Warnow and his orchestra and were entertained by the "Hit Parade." They were kept informed of the news by Edward R. Murrow, Ned Kalmer, Henry Cassidy, Frank McCall, Eric Sevareid, Merrill Mueller, George Hicks, George Thomas Tolster, W. W. Chaplin, Bert Silen, and many others. Kate Smith was selling war bonds, speaking every fifteen minutes on four different days from eight o'clock in the morning till past midnight.

When the French luxury liner *Normandie* burned and capsized at its New York pier in 1942, NBC reporters were on the spot to bring the story to the nation.

The Presidential election of 1940 found radio covering all aspects of the exciting political event. When a "spontaneous" demonstration swept Wendell L. Willkie into the Republican nomination for President, his Midwestern voice became a familiar one to the millions of radio listeners.

"Coming, Mother!" Ezra Stone played the role of cracked-voiced "Henry Aldrich" in "The Aldrich Family." Based on the Broadway hit, *What a Life!,* "The Aldrich Family" was perhaps radio's most successful situation comedy series.

One of radio's most successful producer-directors, William N. Robson, is here shown directing a broadcast in the distinguished "Columbia Workshop" series. Robson also produced such long-time favorites as "Suspense."

One of the early crime series on radio concerned "Mister District Attorney," whose sworn duty was to uphold law and order.

Andre Kostelanetz established a musical vogue—which persists to the present—for big orchestras and lush arrangements. *(Right)* With Metropolitan Opera star Grace Moore.

Arthur Godfrey, who made his first appearance on radio in 1929 on a Baltimore amateur hour, began to attract audience attention in 1934 when he joined WTOP, a CBS station in Washington, as an announcer. Godfrey, the son of a newspaper man, had served in the Navy and Coast Guard, had been a salesman of cemetery lots and finally ended up in show business when a customer sold him half interest in a vaudeville show. Before joining WTOP, Godfrey did a commercial program for a pet shop on station WFBR in Baltimore and was billed as "Red Godfrey, the Warbling Banjoist." After intensive plugging by Walter Winchell in 1941, Godfrey hit the big time on New York's CBS station. Since that time, he has become one of radio's and television's great performers and leading salesman. *(Top, left)* On a morning show in the early 1930's. *(Below)* The first broadcast of "Arthur Godfrey Time" in 1941. The girl at the microphone is singer Patty Clayton. In 1960, "Arthur Godfrey Time" was still a morning favorite.

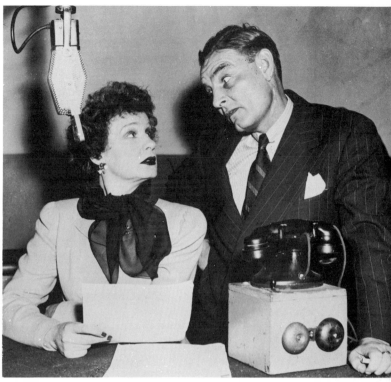

Ed Gardner created the role of Archie in "Duffy's Tavern," a popular show of the 1940's. With him, as Miss Duffy, was Shirley Booth, before she became the great star of stage and screen she is today.

Earl Wilson dubbed the new crooner sensation "Swoonatra," as hysterical screams and "fainting" swept his female audience. Frank Sinatra, who resembled an undernourished schoolboy, sang his way to astronomical popularity. At New York's Paramount Theatre in 1943, the "Voice," as he was called, caused frenzied outbursts in the teen-age audience. His eight-week run at the Riobamba Night Club forced the management to turn away huge crowds. In Hollywood, he made a movie and then returned triumphantly to New York's lush Wedgewood Room of the Waldorf-Astoria. The next step, of course, was radio, a stint on "Your Hit Parade," and his own "Frank Sinatra Show" which brought his voice and personality to countless millions.

Ed Sullivan's interview programs started back in the early 1940's. This picture shows Sullivan interviewing on his program, "Ed Sullivan Entertains."

Probably the most popular figure of the era of the big swing bands was Glenn Miller. A major in the United States Army Air Forces during World War II, he disappeared on a flight in 1944. Miller records, many of them taken from his broadcasts, are still much in demand.

Benny Goodman, the "King of Swing," was one of the top figures of the "big band" era. A gifted clarinetist, Goodman has also worked in the classical field.

Tom Howard, George Shelton, Lulu McConnell and Harry McNaughton in a comedy sketch.

Popular personalities moved from one medium to another. "Blondie and Dagwood," made famous in the syndicated comic strip by Chic Young, moved into radio, starring Arthur Lake and Penny Singleton, who also played the roles in the movies.

Phil Spitalny enchanted his radio fans with his "All Girl" group and sky-rocketed to success as early as 1929.

Lucy Monroe, whose rendition of "The Star Spangled Banner" was world famous, was a hit singer on radio in the 1940's, specializing in semi-classics.

"What's new on the Hollywood scene?" Jimmy Fidler established a reputation for "scooping" the country on personalized news about motion picture stars.

"Your Hit Parade" surveyed phonograph record and sheet-music sales all over the nation and presented the top tunes of the week every Saturday night. It was a big, brassy, breathless show, made more so for many years by the chant of tobacco auctioneer L. A. "Speed" Riggs. Here musical conductor Mark Warnow rehearses Frank Sinatra, who starred on the show in 1943. A season later, Metropolitan Opera star Lawrence Tibbett was the featured singer.

In 1933.

With Garry Moore in 1943.

Jimmy Durante's hoarse voice has been familiar to radio listeners since 1933. A show business veteran, Durante worked his way up from Coney Island honky-tonks to the Broadway stage and Hollywood. He achieved his biggest radio success when he teamed up with Garry Moore during the World War II years.

An excerpt from one of those shows:

MOORE: Now Jimmy, you and I are college students.

DURANTE: Ah, college students.

MOORE: Yes, I'll never forget my first day at school. I went to kindergarten in Baltimore.

DURANTE: I went to kindergarten in Brooklyn.

MOORE: I went to grammar school in Baltimore.

DURANTE: I went to grammar school in Brooklyn.

MOORE: And I graduated.

DURANTE: *Too much education is a dangerous thing.*

"Fibber McGee and Molly" moved into the number two place in 1942, with Jack Benny, Chase and Sanborn, Edgar Bergen and Bob Hope following.

"Abie's Irish Rose" and "The Great Gildersleeve" were moving up. 1943 saw the beginning of a program which was to make radio history. It was called "Take It or Leave it," and gave away the huge sum of $64.00. This program enjoyed the distinction of being the first quiz show to make the top twenty, and popularized the expression "the sixty-four-dollar question." (Later on, in 1956, a new television program was launched and, reflecting inflation, was called "The Sixty-Four-Thousand-Dollar Question"!) The country was also listening to Abbott and Costello. Groucho Marx and Jimmy Durante moved into the top group of audience popularity, and "Grand Ole Op'ry" came into national prominence. The program "Mr. and Mrs. North" was thrilling America with murder and mystery.

1943 also emerged as the year during which NBC sold the Blue Network to Edward J. Noble. Venerable WJZ was one of the key stations in the sale. The event marked the birth of the American Broadcasting Company. Later, in 1953, ABC merged with United Paramount Theatres to form a new corporation, American Broadcasting-Paramount Theatres.

Bud Abbott and Lou Costello were popular radio comedians as early as 1939. The team, which started in burlesque, moved into vaudeville and then motion pictures in the late 1930's. Their humor relies essentially on "corn" and slapstick. An example of Abbott and Costello humor:

ABBOTT: Where have you been Costello? Your clothes are all mussed up. You look like you haven't slept all night.
COSTELLO: I haven't. I can't find any place to live. I sat up all night in the park, and this morning I had to get out of there.

ABBOTT: You had to get out of the park?
COSTELLO: Yeah, the pigeons gave me 24 hours to get a room.
ABBOTT: It's a wonder you didn't freeze to death sleeping in the park.
COSTELLO: Well, I had my little portable radio with me. That keeps me warm.
ABBOTT: Now, how can a radio keep you warm?
COSTELLO: I tune in on Gabriel Heatter.

This picture shows Abbott and Costello guesting on the Fred Allen Show.

In 1943, radio reported to the world the Roosevelt-Churchill Conference at Casablanca. Naples, Italy, broadcast to the United States for the first time since the start of the war.

Bob Hope, who had returned from a world-wide tour of the service camps (which he continued to make all the war years and well into the post-war years), moved into first place in 1944. "Fibber McGee and Molly" were second and Walter Winchell moved up to tie with Jack Benny for third place. Other names and programs which became popular in 1944 were "The Life of Riley," "Truth or Consequences," "Corliss Archer," "Nick Carter" and "Dunninger, the Mind Reader."

By 1944, almost 900 radio stations were in operation throughout the country. CBS and NBC were battling for No. 1 network position. In June all commercial broadcasts were cancelled so that uninterrupted reports might be made on the landing of American troops on the beaches of Normandy. The nation was stirred by reports of successful Allied operations. The invasion, the break-through, the drive on Paris, the second landing on the southern coast of France, all were reported to a waiting world.

*"Good evening, anybody . . ."* Radio's bad boy, Henry Morgan, first became nationally known on a five-night-a-week Mutual series called "Here's Morgan." Then as now, Morgan featured a zany, irreverent brand of humor that frequently got him in trouble with sponsors and networks.

Screen star Rita Hayworth was one of the Hollywood stars appearing on a special full-hour program which dedicated CBS's Latin American network.

Dunninger performed as a radio mind reader in early 1945.

Basil Rathbone achieved the same identification with the role of "Sherlock Holmes" on radio that William Gillette did in an earlier era on the stage. The late Nigel Bruce was his "Dr. Watson."

Red Skelton, the popular comedian, appeared on CBS radio for many years. Skelton built his popularity on gag material such as the material below.

An example of Skelton humor:

SKELTON: My electric toaster broke down, so I repaired it with parts from an airplane.

STOOGE: How's it work out?

SKELTON: Not bad, except now when the toast pops out, it circles the table twice before coming in for a landing.

Dramatic roles in radio used increasing numbers of Hollywood stars. This photograph shows Marlene Dietrich and Ray Milland starring on one of ABC's dramatic programs.

*(Left)* Toscanini conducts the NBC Symphony. *(Right)* Bruno Walter conducts the New York Philharmonic-Symphony.

John Nesbitt *(seated)*, conductor Victor Young, and singer John Charles Thomas on the Westinghouse Sunday concert in 1945.

Serious music came into its own on radio during the 1940's. Most distinguished musical events of the week on network radio were the Sunday afternoon broadcasts of the New York Philharmonic-Symphony on CBS, the Saturday night NBC Symphony programs under Arturo Toscanini and the Saturday afternoon Metropolitan Opera broadcasts on the Blue (now ABC) Network.

In 1944, America experienced another Presidential election. Richard Harkness covered the Democratic Convention for NBC in 1944.

The networks covered the event more extensively than ever before. Here the Blue Network chalks up returns.

The Republican Convention of 1944 provided Herbert Hoover (being introduced by Joe Martin) as the featured speaker.

Bernard Herrmann is shown conducting the Columbia Broadcasting Symphony on "Gateway to Music," a weekly feature in 1945. Herrmann made a tremendous contribution toward the development of a musical idiom for radio, particularly in the field of dramatic background music.

Ruth Douglas, Whitey Ford, Bill Monroe and Roy Acuff, NBC radio stars on the "Grand Ole Op'ry," helped to publicize the American Second War Loan Drive in Nashville. They are shown here inviting buyers to autograph bombs which were destined for Tokyo.

Jane, Helen and Patty Pickens on a 1945 CBS radio broadcast. The three sisters set a pattern of singing style still imitated today. Jane Pickens later became a singing star in her own right.

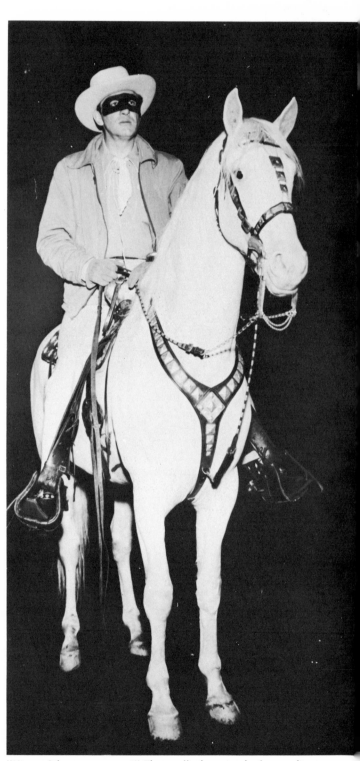

Henry Hull, famous Broadway actor, and star of "Tobacco Road," as he appeared in the CBS series, "Suspense."

"Hi-yo, Silver . . . away!" That call, the sound of pounding hooves, and the pulsing rhythms of the "William Tell Overture" introduced every episode of the Lone Ranger. The adventures of this masked righter-of-wrongs began on Detroit's WXYZ in 1934. Astride his faithful horse Silver in this picture is the Lone Ranger of 1945, Brace Beem.

In the mid-1940's, "You Bet Your Life," starring Groucho Marx, the great vaudeville and screen comic, had already hit the top 20. Marx's fast moving, machine gun type of humor established an excellent reputation for him as a leading comedian in America. An example of Groucho's humor:

Groucho, after receiving applause from the audience: "I would feel flattered at that reception, except that I know you are applauding to keep your hands warm. To come here from California, I was on a train for two days from Chicago, and had to wait eight hours for a plane, and it took another five hours to get here. I think I ought to get a little more applause than that. . . . Good. Even NBC knows the secret word tonight is CBS. . . . And if anybody here says the secret word, don't bother to turn in your expense account."

The pleasant voice and guitar playing of Phil Cook pleased daytime audiences in 1945.

Burl Ives was a popular radio performer and singer of folk tunes in the mid-1940's. His "Burl Ives Show" was a high-rated program.

Bud Collyer, later a popular television M.C., and Billie Burke discuss a script of the "Billie Burke Show," heard on CBS in 1945.

Bandleader Harry James ("You Made Me Love You") had his own show on the Mutual network in 1946.

The Latin-American artist, Juan Arvizu, with the CBS Pan-American Orchestra, conductd by Alfredo Antonini.

Marie Wilson and Alan Reed as they appeared in the popular situation comedy, "My Friend Irma," in the late 1940's. "Irma" was later a TV favorite, too.

Jack Bailey was master of ceremonies on "Queen for a Day," a daytime women's show. He is shown receiving an award from editor Evelyn Bixby, of *Radio Life*, in 1946.

Robert Montgomery narrating on a CBS "Suspense" program.

Xavier Cugat was a regular on "Spotlight Bands" via Mutual in 1946.

Thomas E. Dewey, Presidential hopeful, speaks to reporters after learning of his defeat at the polls in 1948. In the background is Jim Hagerty, then Dewey's press representative.

On April 12, 1945, a short flash came through to the network news rooms which said, "Washington—F.D.R. dead." John Daly and others reported to the country that the President had died of a cerebral hemorrhage at Warm Springs, Georgia, and that Mrs. Roosevelt had called Vice-President Truman to the White House to inform him of the occurrence. All commercial broadcasting was cancelled from April 12 to the 15th and programs were restricted to appropriate news and memorials. An announcer named Arthur Godfrey made a memorable broadcast of the funeral procession.

On May 7, the Associated Press sent a radio flash from Rheims, France, "The Allies officially announce that Germany has unconditionally surrendered." The war in Europe was over.

Later in August, Max Joran of NBC, broadcasting from Basel, Switzerland, told of the arrival of Japanese surrender papers, and on September 1, 1945, radio reported "on-the-spot" descriptions of the Japanese surrender on the U.S.S. "Missouri" in Tokyo Bay.

At the end of World War II in 1945, performers were returning from war duty and several revisions were made in the popularity polls. Red Skelton had moved up to seventh place. Rudy Vallee was back in the running. New programs on the air included "The Danny Kaye Show" and "Beulah."

In 1946 Jack Benny made a comeback, moving once again into first place, and Fanny Brice was still a strong contender in the Hooper rating system. In 1947, the list of names in the top twenty remained virtually unchanged, with some minor exceptions. Marie Wilson had entered the group with her "My Friend, Irma." Also new and destined to skyrocket to popularity was Arthur Godfrey's "Talent Scouts."

In 1948, Walter Winchell garnered first position. "Lux Radio Theatre" took second place with "My Friend, Irma" moving up to sixth. "Duffy's Tavern" was in seventh place and Arthur Godfrey in eighth. Tenth place was held by Phil Harris and Alice Faye.

The 1940's saw radio mature into a stable, prosperous medium with a developing complacency and a gradual orderly increase in station competition. The period also witnessed an increase in government surveillance and a public awareness of the tremendous influence of radio. As the decade drew to a close, changes were taking place that were to have the greatest impact on the country's listening habits—a sudden increase in the number of stations . . . sharper competition . . . the re-introduction of F.M. . . . and the growth of television.

In 1946, Martha Rountree and Lawrence Spivak founded a new, dynamic and unrehearsed program called, "Meet the Press." The program subjected national and international personalities to penetrating questions by some of the country's ablest journalists. It brought to millions of radio listeners and later to television viewers, the exciting drama inherent in the "give and take" which occurs when the press seeks answers to important questions. Here James Roosevelt (extreme right) is being quizzed by the panel.

Reaching its height in popularity in the late 1940's, "America's Town Meeting of the Air" brought provocative discussions to the radio audience. Shown here (left to right) in a program entitled "Let's Face the Race Question" are John Temple Graves, George V. Denny, Jr., director of the program, Langston Hughes and Carey Williams.

A comedy show on WOR which featured Arnold Stang.

Radio fans followed the Alice Faye-Phil Harris romance eagerly and were happy when it culminated in a successful marriage. Harris was a veteran radio bandleader, having achieved his greatest renown on the Jack Benny shows. Alice Faye had been a radio singer and was a top motion picture star, In the years following World War II, they had a weekly comedy show of their own.

"Martin Kane, Private Eye," starred William Gargan, Mary Orr and Mitzi Gould on WOR-Mutual in 1949.

The "First Nighter" dramas were a highly popular series in 1947—as they had been for many years before. Olan Soule and Barbara Luddy were co-stars in the program which was aired from the mythical "Little Theater Off Times Square."

The "Family Theater" was a popular WOR-Mutual program utilizing Hollywood stars such as Gene Lockhart and Ruth Hussey; shown with them is father Patrick C. Payton. *(Left)* Errol Flynn in a "Family Theater" broadcast.

John B. Kennedy was a mutual newscaster in the late 1940's.

J. Carrol Naish played the main role in the popular radio program "Life with Luigi."

Eve Arden's role as a wise-cracking school teacher in the "Our Miss Brooks" program started and maintained its popularity on radio. Here, we see Eve Arden, Dick Crenna and Gloria McMillan performing on CBS.

Garry Moore and Bill Comstock on the "Garry Moore Show" in 1949. Comstock may be portraying "Lizzie Tish," a character he created for the "Al Pearce Show" in the late thirties.

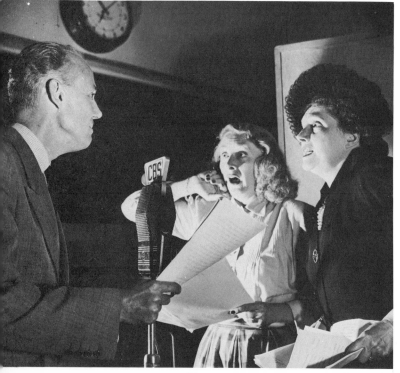

Mystery programs like "Inner Sanctum" were still popular radio fare in 1949. Vera Allen, Arlene Blackburn and Frank Mellow are shown on an "Inner Sanctum" broadcast.

"Alka Seltzer Time" featured Herb Shriner with his dry and subtle humor.

On the "Quiz Kids" broadcasts, a kind of juvenile "Information Please," brainy youngsters answered questions that stumped most of their adult listeners. Clifton Fadiman was moderator.

Begun in 1930, the prize-winning fantasy series "Let's Pretend" was still going strong in 1948. Shown above *(left)* are Owen Davies, Butch Cavell, Bill Lipton, and Sybil Trent in a broadcast of that year. Below is an early picture of Nila Mack, originator of the series, and some of the children who appeared in it.

In 1949 the "Lum and Abner" radio series was still a very popular show. Starring in the program were Chet Lauck, as Lum, and Norris Goff, as Abner. *(Left)* Before the mike with comedienne ZaSu Pitts. *(Right)* Made up for their rustic roles.

The late Al Jolson visits the Bing Crosby show in 1949.

Frank Singeiser reports the news for Mutual in 1949.

*Part Five:* THE FIFTIES

8:30 **MEASURE FOR MEASURE:** the BBC production of Shakespeare's "dark" comedy, with Michael Horden, Deryck Guyler and Hermione Hannen in the cast. **(MAY 24)**

10:30 **CHAMBER CONCERT:** (May 18)

## SUNDAY, May 22

8:00 **ORCHESTRAL-CHORAL CONCERT**
FRANCAIX Concertino for Piano
(Weber, Berlin Sym—Fricsay) (Decca 9900) (9)
MOZART Symphony No. 25, G minor, K. 183
(London Sym—Solti) (Lon 1034) (18)
BERLIOZ Les Nuits d'Ete
(de los Angeles, Boston—Munch) (Vic 1907) (31)
BEETHOVEN Piano Concerto No. 1, C minor
(de Groot, Vienna Sym—Otterloo) (Epic 3434) (34)
POULENC Stabat Mater
(Chorus, Colonne Orch—Fremaux) (West 18422) (24)

10:00 **BOOKS:** Kenneth Rexroth in his weekly program of review and comment.

10:30 **REPORT TO THE LISTENER:** (May 19)

10:45 **PIANO RECITAL:** (April 11)
SATIE: Three Pieces in the Form of a Pear
PROKOFIEV Sonata No. 7, B♭, Op. 83
BARTOK Mikrokosmos, Vol. 4
ROZSA Piano Sonata (1948)

11:45 **PEACETIME USES OF NUCLEAR ENERGY:** fifth in a series of talks produced by KPFA. Tonight we hear Jerome Kohl, Tracerlab, Inc., on nuclear energy, electronics and automation.

12:00 **FOLKSINGER'S CHOICE:** Folk music, live and recorded, with Cynthia Gooding. **(MAY 24)**

1:00 **THE GREAT ANTAGONISTS:** Jefferson and Marshall. First of three talks by Julian Parks Boyd, author, educator and editor. **(MAY 23)**

2:00 **REGINA:** Marc Blitzstein's three-act opera based on Lillian Hellman play "The Little Foxes." Brenda Lewis sings the title role, with Carol Bruce as Addie, Elizabeth Carron as Birdie and Joshua Hecht as Horace. Samuel Krachmalnick conducts the N.Y.C. Opera Orchestra and Chorus. Marc Blitzstein and Brenda Lewis will be interviewed between acts by Gene Bruck. **(MAY 25)**

4:30 **THE THEATRE:** an informal discussion among David Susskind, Kenneth Tynan and Gore Vidal. **(MAY 17)**

5:30 **MISCELLANY**

6:00 **LEARNING TO LIVE IN A NEW KIND OF WORLD:** Dr. C. Brock Chisholm, Canadian psychiatrist and former head of World Health Organization, talks on the contribution of the social sciences toward a better understanding of ourselves, our world and our need to adapt for survival. **(MAY 27)**

7:00 **CRITIC AT LARGE:** James Lyons.

7:30 **NEW RECORDINGS**

8:00 **THE FILM ART:** Gideon Bachmann interviews Leslie Stevens, producer-director, on the subject "Is There A New Wave in American Film Making?" **(MAY 26)**

8:45 **BUDAPEST HAYDN FESTIVAL, 1959:** third in a series of concerts distributed by the BFA. Tonight, a concert by the Pasquier String Trio. **(MAY 27)**
HAYDN Three Divertimenti
LASZLO LAJTHA Trio No. 2
BEETHOVEN Trio, C minor, Op. 3, No. 2

10:00 **THE SCOPE OF JAZZ:** Nat Hentoff and Martin Williams discuss the jazz scene and play records.

11:30 **PARIS SPOTLIGHT:** a weekly program describing events and life in Paris, produced for Pacifica by the French Radio.

## MONDAY, May 23

8:00 **ORCHESTRAL CONCERT**
BACH Violin Concerto, E major
(Ayo, I Musici) (Epic 3553) (20)
SCHUMANN Symphony No. 3, E♭ major "Rhenish"
(Paris Conserv—Schuricht) (Lon 1037) (29)
BOCCHERINI Symphony, C minor
(Philharmonia—Guilini) (Ang 35712) (12)
RACHMANINOFF Piano Concerto No. 3, D minor
(Schein, Vienna Orch—Goossens) (Kapp 6000) (42)

9:55 **NEWS**

10:00 **THE GREAT ANTAGONISTS:** (May 22)

11:00 **LIEGE MUSIC FESTIVAL:** (May 18)

12:30 **POETRY READ BY DAVID ALLEN:** (May 18)

1:00 **THE CREATIVE MIND:** Milton Nahm, Louis Finkelstein and Reinhold Neibuhr on "Man the Creator." (May 19)

1:30 **LIBRARY OF CONGRESS CONCERT:** (May 20)

3:30 **THE GRADUATE SERIES OF THE NEW YORK ACADEMY OF MEDICINE:** (May 18)

4:25 **THEATRE SERVICE**

4:30 **PROGRAMS FOR CHILDREN**
Around Africa: On the Island of Madagascar
Folksongs
The White Deer: part three, read by Mike Tigar.

5:30 **WANDA LANDOWSKA RECITAL:** (April 20)
MOZART Piano Sonata, B♭ major, K. 333
BACH Harpsichord Concerto, D minor

6:30 **NEWS**

6:45 **COMMENTARY:** Michael Scriven. **(MAY 24)**

7:00 **FOLK MUSIC ABROAD:** Henrietta Yurchenko.

7:30 **PHILOSOPHY EAST AND WEST:** Alan W. Watts, noted Asia scholar, in his weekly series of talks on Asian philosophy and its contemporary impact. **(MAY 26)**

8:00 **FURTWAENGLER FESTIVAL:** nineteenth in the series of concerts of recordings made by the late Wilhelm Furtwaengler.
MOZART Serenade No. 10, B♭ major, K. 361
(Vienna Philharmonic Wind Ensemble) (HMV)
WAGNER Excerpts from Die Gotterdammerung
(Vienna Philharmonic) (Electrola)

9:00 **CAPITAL PUNISHMENT:** Dr. Austin McCormick, Dean of the University of California School of Criminology. **(MAY 29)**

9:30 **W. H. AUDEN:** the poet reading from his own work, recorded in the WBAI studios. (May 15)

10:00 **REPORT ON MUSIC:** Gene Bruck. **(MAY 24)**

11:30 **JAZZ CONCERT**

## TUESDAY, May 24

8:00 **CONCERT OF CONTEMPORARY MUSIC**
SHOSTAKOVITCH Ballet Suite No. 2
(USSR State Orch—Gauk) (CE 3012) (12)
BLOCH Schelomo
(Neikrug, Symphony of Air—Stokowski) (UA 7005) (22)
STRAVINSKY Concerto for Two Pianos
(Brendel, Zelka, SWO Orch—Byrns) (Vox 10660) (21)
HONEGGER Symphony No. 5
(Lamoureux—Markevitch) (Decca 9956) (23)
ORFF Catulli Carmina
(Soloists, Choir, Ens—Jochum (Decca 9824) (35)

9:55 **NEWS**

10:00 **COMMENTARY:** Michael Scriven. (May 23)

10:15 **MEASURE FOR MEASURE (BBC):** May 21

12:15 **REPORT ON MUSIC:** Gene Bruck. (May 23)

1:45 **NYASALAND'S STRUGGLE FOR INDEPENDENCE:** Dr. Hastings Banda. (May 19)

A promising development of the 1950's was listener-subscription radio, or "voluntary listener-sponsorship," as it is described by Pacifica Foundation, which pioneered the idea at KPFA in Berkeley, California. Under this system, a frankly highbrow program schedule, including classical music, jazz, lectures, plays, poetry readings, etc., is offered completely free of commercial sponsorship. Costs are borne by the listeners, who contribute a minimum of twelve dollars a year. This is in no way comparable to the various toll schemes that have been advanced over the years for both radio and television, for listeners who subscribe do so completely altruistically—anyone with an FM receiver can tune in for nothing. Oddly enough, the plan is working. Pacifica now has three stations—the original KPFA, KPFK in Los Angeles, and WBAI in New York.

The schedule shown here, a typical page from the program folio of Station WBAI, shows the high level of programming possible under this system.

"The Big Show," a lavish 90-minute weekly variety program, was launched on November 4, 1950. With Tallulah Bankhead as hostess and Meredith Willson as musical director, it featured the biggest stars in show business. In this picture are, left to right, George Sanders, Portland Hoffa, Groucho Marx, Fred Allen, and Tallulah.

# The Fifties

1950 was the year of coming-of-age for television and a year of diminishing activity for radio. It was the year that President Truman instructed the Atomic Energy Commission to produce the hydrogen bomb. It was the year that Jerusalem was proclaimed capital of Israel. In 1950, the Republic of Korea was invaded by the Communists and President Truman and General Douglas MacArthur conferred on Wake Island. On November 1, 1950, two Puerto Rican fanatics tried unsuccessfully to shoot their way into the President's house. The United States banned shipments to the China mainland. President Truman proclaimed a state of National Emergency calling for a united effort to withstand Communist aggression.

1950 was a major year for television. It was a year of big names, bigger programs and new studios. The Nielsen Ratings, which had taken over from Hooper, indicated that while television was a fast-growing

youth, radio remained a healthy adult. Tallulah Bankhead defied television with her big Sunday night radio program, "The Big Show," on NBC.

The complexion of radio, however, was rapidly changing. Evening audiences in increasingly greater numbers switched to television, although the radio daytime audiences were maintained. In 1950, radio programs such as "Fibber McGee and Molly," Judy Canova, "Mr. District Attorney," Bob Hope and "The Great Gildersleeve" were still enticing large listening audiences.

The decline of network radio during this period was marked. Television had advanced rapidly during its short nine years of commercial existence, forcing radio to undergo some painful and fundamental changes. The big audience had moved over to television, particularly during the most lucrative evening hours. Radio, which had become accustomed to total home

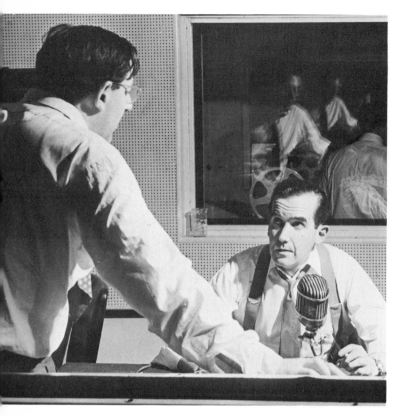

"Hear It Now," produced by Fred W. Friendly and Edward R. Murrow was an excellent radio documentary series that foreshadowed the same team's "See It Now" on television.

"Songs for Sale," with Jan Murray (*right*) as host, offered aspiring songwriters a showcase for their work in 1951.

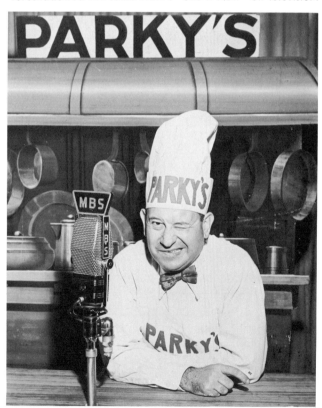

Comedian "Parkyakarkus," a veteran of the Eddie Cantor shows of the 1930's, had his own program in 1952.

J. Edgar Hoover, the F.B.I. chief, frequently appeared on radio in behalf of the nation's fight against organized crime.

Singing sensation Eddie Fisher (another of Eddie Cantor's protégés) here sings on the "Time for Defense" show during his hitch in the U.S. Army in 1951.

People were funny in 1951, as "People Are Funny" today. Art Linkletter starred in this program on radio and later on TV. Linkletter also presides over the popular daytime "House Party."

audiences during its first days, had to satisfy itself with the left-overs consisting of those families which did not have TV sets, those which did not like the TV programs being offered, and automobile listeners. As the radio audience grew smaller, competition to win the available listening public intensified. Radio was forced to economize greatly and new program formats emerged. Music and news which had become the standby of the smaller independent stations were now adopted by the networks. Indeed, the very existence of the radio network structure became threatened as its satellite stations discovered that a central organization could no longer provide attractive programming which the local station itself could not do as well.

But radio was *not* dying as many had predicted it would; instead it was changing its pattern. In 1959, about 156,000,000 radio receivers were in working condition in the United States, more than three times the number of TV sets. Twenty-six per cent of these were in automobiles, and the rest were in homes—not necessarily in the living room, but scattered throughout the house from cellar to attic. It appeared that radio was drawing audiences as large as ever at times when television could not comfortably be viewed. Radio listening, not requiring complete attention, was maintaining the interest of the housewife during the hours·when she cleaned her home, when she ate, when she and her family were out driving.

An ingenious flexibility in network programming was introduced by NBC in 1955 with the 40-hour weekend show, "Monitor," which provided for network programming with both local and national spot advertising. "Monitor" represented a new concept in radio, with its combination of interviews, remote pick-ups, comedy briefs, music, and news. It eliminated the former set time periods, and worked on a "as long as necessary" basis.

The stiff competition of television in the 1950's forced other networks and stations to provide more "service" programming and programs of the kind television "could not do well." A greater emphasis was placed on radio's mobility, with more frequent on-the-spot news coverage, the use of travelling transmitters in cars, planes, and helicopters. The vast car-radio audience began to receive special attention, with frequent traffic condition reports, etc.

The "disc jockey" became a figure to reckon with in the 1950's. Originally simply a radio announcer who played phonograph records, the "disc jockey" built up

Radio still did its most exciting performances with on-the-spot interviews. Ben Grauer, a leading NBC commentator and veteran performer, is shown interviewing individuals in a crowd of New Yorkers.

One of England's great comediennes, Gracie Fields, headlined her own "Gracie Fields Show" on the Mutual Network in 1951.

One of the most popular cowboys in entertainment history —William Boyd as "Hopalong Cassidy."

In 1952 Steve Allen, with his CBS radio show, "The Steve Allen Show," had achieved a high degree of popularity. Allen, in his half-hour show of casual and relaxed comedy, presented both music and well-known stars. A talented musician and writer, Allen is the author of a number of best-selling books and popular songs. He was born in 1921, the only child of two vaudeville comedians. After attending Arizona State Teachers' College, he broke into radio as announcer on a local station and gained a wide radio following, working up from routine announcing jobs into full-fledged comedy programs.

huge followings who were attracted to him because of his personality and the kind of music he played. The format of the disc jockey show—music and patter— made it ideal for spot advertising, before, after, and sometimes even during records. With the virtual demise of "live" music on radio, the disc jockeys, such as Art Ford, Martin Block (who with his "Make-Believe Ballroom" was a pioneer in this form), Jerry Marshal and scores of others almost control the commercial music field.

The activities of the disc jockey came under public scrutiny in late 1959, after the television quiz show scandals cast suspicion on the whole broadcasting industry. Investigations by the Federal Communications Commission uncovered widespread use of the "plug" and "payola" in radio. The plug involved payment of as high as a thousand dollars for the mention of a product on a high-rated program; payola was the special compensation payed to disc jockeys for pushing specific recordings. As much as $20,000 was paid

Georgia Gibbs, Johnny Johnston and Vera Ellen, appeared on the program "The M.G.M. Musical Comedy Theater" on Mutual in 1952.

In 1952, the program "Grand Central Station" maintained its radio popularity. Producer Martin Horrell boosted many of his radio players to Hollywood stardom. He appears in the above picture with Neva Patterson, a popular "Grand Central Station" performer.

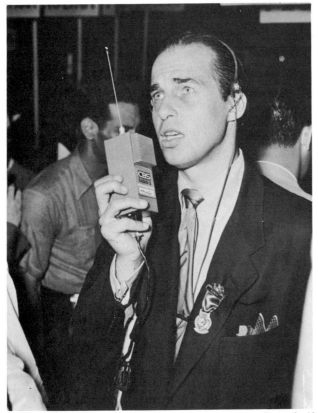

CBS radio newsman Allen Jackson, with a five and one-half pound walkie-talkie transmitter, broadcast the story of the Republican Convention in July, 1952.

Brightest comics to emerge in radio's postwar years are Bob (Elliott) & Ray (Goulding). Two of their many voices are familiar to TV viewers as those of "Bert and Harry" in the popular beer commercials.

*"Back in the saddle again. . ."* Movie cowboy Gene Autry was a hit on radio too.

Alan Freed, whose disc jockey activities helped popularize "rock 'n' roll" music, suspended his career during the 1960 Federal investigation of "payola" scandals.

by one record company to popularize a "best sellin" tune.

Congress finally came into the picture in November of 1959. A House Subcommittee on Legislative Oversight, shocked into action by public indignation, dug into facts embarrassing to FCC officials, who had long neglected proper controls.

Highly unethical radio station activities all over the country were discovered. In Detroit, for example, two stations openly plugged a song for the "right price." In Chicago, major disc jockeys frankly sought out payola opportunities. Important disc jockeys were often made part-owners of producing companies, thereby assuring continuous plugging of the company's songs. A record company in Philadelphia admitted that it had twenty-five local disc jockeys on a regular monthly payroll, ranging from $25 to $200 each. Con-

gress quickly passed stringent legislation designed to curb such activities.

A program form that has been extremely successful in the 1950's is the radio documentary, its versimilitude made possible by the tape recorder. Such broadcasts as NBC's "Biographies in Sound," which profiled great contemporaries in the words and voices of their friends and acquaintances, and "Image Russia," which

Gayelord Hauser imparted health information and dieting advice to millions of listeners throughout the country.

CBS sports reporter Red Barber provided many exciting play-by-play descriptions of major league baseball games throughout the country.

Lowell Thomas, who substituted for Floyd Gibbons one night in 1930 and went on to more than a quarter of a century of topnotch news broadcasting.

The famed denizens of "Allen's Alley" pose for their picture on the occasion of NBC's 30th anniversary in 1956. Left to right, Fred Allen; "Senator Claghorn" (Kenny Delmar); "Mrs. Nussbaum" (Minerva Pious); "Ajax Cassidy" (Peter Donald); and "Titus Moody" (Parker Fenelly).

gave an exhaustive treatment to the Soviet Union, and CBS's special reports such as "Who Killed Michael Farmer?," "The Galindez Case," and "The Business of Sex" have brought critical acclaim, good audience response, and wide attention in the press.

The 1950's also saw an increase in the number of independent stations that specialized in classical music and other "highbrow" material. Usually broadcasting on F.M., these stations often made a special bid for the attention of high-fidelity sound enthusiasts.

A new development that seems likely to increase in importance is stereophonic broadcasting. Up till now, the stereophonic effect has been achieved by the sta-tion's broadcasting the two sound channels (or "sides") on its A.M. and F.M. transmitters respectively and the listener's tuning in on his A.M. and F.M. receivers, appropriately placed for the most realistic effect, but a new form of "multiplex" broadcasting will permit both channels to go out over a single F.M. wavelength. A special receiver will be required, of course.

So radio goes on, and contrary to the predictions of a decade ago, is likely to go on for a long time to come. Its glamorous days gone forever, it remains the medium the most people turn to for news, service programs, and music. It is the nation's bulletin board and everybody's music box.

Veteran radio quizmaster and comedian Walter O'Keefe became summer-time host on the CBS radio program "Two For The Money" in 1954, while regular moderator Herb Shriner vacationed.

James Cagney as he re-created his role of George M. Cohan in the "Screen Guild Players" production of *Yankee Doodle Dandy in 1952.*

Both radio and television gave exhaustive coverage to the Coronation of Elizabeth II in 1953. Background interviews, such as the one shown above, brought Howard K. Smith, a CBS radio correspondent, into contact with interesting members of the British public.

The "Dr. Christian" program, starring Jean Hersholt, was one of the few radio programs which encouraged new writing talent. The program offered special prizes for best dramatic scripts written by non-professionals, and is credited with having discovered many leading radio and television writers.

"Andy Hardy" came to radio intact from the screen and starred Lewis Stone and Mickey Rooney.

Homespun Galen Drake has a wide and loyal following among the nation's housewives.

An intimate atmosphere characterizes "Breakfast with Dorothy and Dick" (Dick Kollmar and Dorothy Kilgallen). The program is broadcast from their New York apartment, the microphones being set on the table among the breakfast dishes. The couple chat naturally about family incidents, plays they have seen, parties they have been to, and people they know. Kollmar has been successful on the musical stage and in films and television, as well as radio. Dorothy Kilgallen, probably the nation's best-known newspaperwoman, is also known to millions of TV viewers as a panelist on "What's My Line?"

This husband and wife formula has been very effective in radio, other notables in the field being Tex McCrary and Jinx Falkenburg and the Fitzgeralds, Ed and Pegeen.

Rosemary Clooney and Bing Crosby duet on their Monday-through-Friday morning show on CBS.

The pleasant, easy-going mannerisms of Jack Sterling make getting up in the morning easier for many New Yorkers.

Bill Stern reports sporting events on WOR.

Peter Lind Hayes and wife Mary Healy, favorites with daytime listeners, here indulge in some horseplay with Mr. John, the hat designer (*center*).

Typical of the wake-up programs that are one of the mainstays of latter-day radio is the "Bill Cullen Show" on WNBC in New York. Here is Bill with Betty Brewer, recording artist and night club singer.

The smooth voice and pleasing personality of Lanny Ross were still winning him listeners in the 1950's, as they did on the old "Maxwell House Showboat."

The thirtieth anniversary of NBC found young and energetic Robert W. Sarnoff as president of the vast organization.

Jean Shepherd, a disc jockey-turned-philosopher whose iconoclastic ramblings attracted a fanatical following in New York.

"Long John" Nebel, whose all-night discussion program on WOR in New York tackles subjects ranging from flying saucers to drug addiction.

"The Happiness Exchange" conducted by Joe Rosenfield, Jr. ("Big Joe"), airs the troubles of listeners and finds assistance for them. In this picture, left to right, are Mary Margaret McBride; "Big Joe"; Taylor Wallace; novelist Fanny Hurst; and Chief Ed Edelman of the Purple Heart. Celebrities often donate their services to "The Happiness Exchange."

In the 1950's radio sought out new audiences in the hours when most television screens were dark. Midnight-to-dawn programs flourished, especially in big cities with their armies of "night people." For the most part, recorded music was the mainstay of these programs, but challenging the sway of the disc jockey were off-beat shows like those above.

One of latter-day radio's biggest boosters is Arthur Godfrey, whose relaxed Monday-through-Friday morning show is a highspot of the CBS schedule. "The joy of this is," Godfrey said recently, "that we get about a thousand letters a week, many from people saying they're rediscovering radio." Here he "noodles around" (his words) with Benny Goodman.

Zany comedian Robert Q. Lewis presided over one of radio's last live comedy shows five nights a week during 1957.

# Part Six: THE SIXTIES

The Negro radio listener was better informed than his predecessors had ever been. This dramatic incident of the civil rights movement received on-the-scene news coverage. James Meredith, the man who broke the racial barrier at the University of Mississippi, was shot and wounded by a segregationist while leading a march through the state. Leaning over him is Sherwood Ross, editorial writer and news correspondent for the Sonderling group of radio stations, who also acted as Meredith's public relations man during the march.

Joe Garagiola typified a new breed of sports broadcaster. Ex-athletes such as Garagiola ("Baseball's most famous .250 hitter"), Phil Rizzuto, Ralph Kiner, Pee Wee Reese, Frank Gifford, and others, replaced established newspaper reporter types such as Mel Allen and Red Barber. Broadcasting's domination of professional sports was highlighted in the 1960's by the CBS purchase of the New York Yankees. (Garagiola with Burt Lancaster, movie actor, on *Monitor*.)

In the 1960's, radio became old enough to look back nostalgically upon its place in history. In 1966 David Sarnoff, chairman of the board of RCA, was honored at a testimonial dinner for his 60 years in communications. The awards are being presented by Lowell Thomas and Frederick A. Kappel, chairman of the American Telephone and Telegraph Company. It was Sarnoff who foresaw the possibilities for radio in the home as early as 1916, and who played a leading role in establishing network radio with formation of NBC in 1926.

# The Sixties

In 1960, network radio finally abandoned the attempt to compete with television in the kind of family entertainment performers call The Big Show. Two last survivors of the great days went off the air: *Amos 'n' Andy* (since 1928) and *National Barn Dance* (since 1932). The advent of color television seemed proof again that whatever radio could do to attract audiences, television could do better. However, events were in motion that would lift voice broadcasting to greater heights of popularity than ever before.

The headlines of 1960 were portentous. On the eve of a peace-making summit conference between President Eisenhower and Premier Khrushchev, an American reconnaissance plane, the U-2, was shot down over the Soviet Union and its pilot imprisoned as a spy. Khrushchev denounced the United States, refused to confer with Eisenhower, and at the United Nations in New York he pounded a desk with his shoe. Cuba's

*Yanqui*-hating Fidel Castro warmly embraced him, as did Egypt's Nasser. There were 17 new African nations and blood-stained terror in the Congo.

The 1960 census placed the population at 179,323,-175. Promising to "get this country moving again," Senator John F. Kennedy won the Democratic nomination for President and narrowly defeated Republican Vice President Richard M. Nixon. Their confrontation on television, watched by 65 million people, was a landmark in American politics and a decisive factor in the election results. After the election, the nation's spirits revived in a glow of New Frontier optimism, little suspecting the tragedy that was to befall its brilliant young leader.

Kennedy's short but scintillating presidency was beset with problems and alarms; the Bay of Pigs disaster in Cuba, followed by Russian missiles on the island and a near-nuclear crisis; civil rights agitation

The constant availability and increasing portability of the radio set itself, thanks to the transistor, created a growing 24-hour-a-day audience of listeners.

Radio responded brilliantly to the emergency during the power blackout on November 6, 1965. Here, Barrie Beere, News Director of WMCA, New York, using special auxiliary equipment, broadcast the news and emergency instructions by candlelight.

in the South followed by the use of armed force to permit a Negro, James Meredith, to enter the University of Mississippi; growing involvement in a seemingly endless war in Vietnam; strikes and a collapse, in 1962, of the long stock market boom. Yet, the President won the hearts of the young, established the Peace Corps, and seemed to have turned the tide of the cold war with the Soviet Union.

Radio played a secondary role to television in influencing these events. As an entertainment medium, it reeled from the shock of the "payola" scandals. Standard Top Forty programming—so-called because stations constantly played the 40 top-ranking hit tunes —was in disrepute. The Federal Trade Commission filed more than 100 complaints of unethical record promotions and "plugging" of other products by disc jockeys. Some of the accused stations, notably WINS, New York, were denied renewal of their licenses.

President Kennedy's chairman of the Federal Communications Commission, Newton N. Minow, labeled television a "vast wasteland" and had equally harsh words for radio. "To twist the radio dial today," he said, "is to be shoved through a bazaar, a clamorous Casbah of pitchmen and commercials which plead, bleat, pressure, whistle, groan, and shout. Too many stations have become publicly franchised jukeboxes."

Continued, though at times uneasy, economic growth and prosperity proved to be radio's saviour. Despite the TV takeover, sales of radio sets boomed

One sign of the upgrading of public musical taste was the popularity of the stereo cartridge tape player for automobiles. With it, a driver could play four numbers of his own selection through the car radio, using an 8-track tape and two to four speakers. FM receivers for cars also appeared, especially in areas where the local AM air waves were dominated by rock 'n' roll or "rockabilly."

WOR, New York, developed the format of the all-talk station over a period of 20 years. Its consistently top or near-top audience ratings led to the discovery of the magic appeal of good conversation by the industry in general, and the trend to talk as the major element in programming. The station's daily schedule is widely imitated.

Helicopter spotting of traffic jams with reporter Fred Feldman made WOR a listening habit for thousands of car-borne commuters each morning and night.

surprisingly after 1955. Ten years later, some 43 million were sold—more than half as many as had existed in 1949, radio's last big pre-television year. Around 242 million were in use, more radios than people, three times the number of telephones. The average household had four sets. The startling fact was that virtually every man, woman, and child in America owned at least one radio set, and that wherever he went, radio went with him.

The clock radio, the battery radio, and the miniature transistor set were popping up in kitchens, bedrooms, on office desks and factory work tables, even in Cossack hats and shirt pockets. While television had indeed taken over the living room, monopolizing family listening, radio had captured the individual.

During the day, comparatively few people have the leisure to watch a television program; for car drivers it would be dangerous. Adult audiences tended to concentrate in the prime evening hours—the same that had given old-time radio its most memorable programs and greatest profits. (Early morning programs and ball games on weekend afternoons were other television peaks.) But people listened to radio *all* day and all night: in cars, in bed, while shaving, at work, at the beach, on boats, in the supermarket . . . or just walking along the street. Sports events presented the phenomenon of the spectator who has paid to watch one game gluing an ear to radio to follow another. Radio became the nation's constant companion.

Ed and Pegeen Fitzgerald specialized on books and authors on WOR. Such cultural or quasi-cultural material did much during the 1960's to win back adult audiences to regular radio listening.

Barry Farber was another talker not content with surface chatter. His formula was to mingle the political with the adventurous: for example, a federal official discussing President Johnson's Great Society followed by an explorer loaded with true adventure tales.

The late George Clay, NBC News correspondent, taping a broadcast for *Monitor*. (Clay was killed by snipers while on assignment in the Congo.) Through the years, this famous weekend show, the pioneer of weekend "talk" shows, has had many newsbeats and exclusive eyewitness reports. For example, James Hagerty, when press secretary to President Eisenhower, learned of the President's heart attack while listening to *Monitor*.

*Monitor*, a revolutionary new concept in weekend programming was the capitalization on what network radio could do best—mobility and immediacy. In ten years *Monitor* achieved an audience of 13 per cent of all adult Americans (15.7 million) and total listenership of about 20 million.

World-wide stories are gathered by NBC newsmen on the spot and phoned to Radio Central in New York, where they are taped for broadcast within seconds, or held for later programming. *Monitor* is heard in five blocks on Saturday and Sunday, totaling 16 hours air time. The Sunday night wrap-up and examination of the week's news has been a frequent Peabody Award winner. The show is one of the most emulated formats in radio, and one of the highest sources of revenue.

Audience researchers took a new look at the "day people," the "night people," and the American on the move indoors and out. The networks, which had been operating in the red since the mid-1950's, became profitable again in 1963. They found imaginative ways to exploit two areas in which television could *not* do better: instantaneous transmission of news, and continuous communication with the listener.

Two events dramatized radio's pervasive reach. On November 22, 1963, President Kennedy was assassinated in Dallas at midday. The news flashed around the country by radio rather than by television. The networks, using an automatic alert system, instantly cut into the programs of all affiliated stations. And people heard. Knots of shocked passersby gathered around car radios in the street, in shops and offices. Within minutes it seemed that everyone knew.

On the night of Tuesday, November 9, 1965, an unprecedented power failure struck seven populous Northeastern states. Everything went dark. People were trapped in pitch black subway tunnels, elevators, unheated and unlighted buildings. No one knew what had happened. But, converting quickly to emergency sources of electricity, radio stations put the facts on the air and were heard by millions. The uninterrupted flow of information was credited with averting panic during the 12 hours of blackout.

In programming for this huge but fragmented and essentially local audience, the networks and major stations took a cue from the smaller independents. A listener on the move must have his attention seized and held. Local station managers aimed at a certain "sound," something unique about the station that would establish an image for its call-letters. In the

effort to create continuous excitement, the Top Forty
format frequently degenerated to a puerile level of
taste. The news shrank into tabloid headlines, and the
platters into mere musical cement between commercials. But the principle was sound; what remained was
to upgrade the contents.

One early reaction to noisy, low-IQ offerings was
the rise of FM—broadcasting sound with a high degree of faithfulness to the original. In 1955 only 38
stations were broadcasting exclusively in the static-
free, high-fidelity band. In the 1960's the number grew
to 1500, including affiliates of AM stations which du-
plicated or "simulcast" the parent programs. It was
the independent FM stations, often sponsored by
churches, universities, or non-profit foundations such
as Pacifica, that learned to cater to the "highbrow"
audience alienated by rock 'n' roll. They found it surprisingly large, loyal, and influential.

In 1961 the FCC established standards for stereo
(multiplex) broadcasting, thus adding classical stereophonic records to FM's fare. The "hi-fi" enthusiast also
was receptive to serious drama, discussions of the arts
and public affairs, and similar intellectual material.
FM radio became a counterpart of England's Third
Program, often rebroadcasting BBC cultural tapes. In
1962 for the first time an FM station (WFMT, Chicago) won the Peabody award for best radio
entertainment.

Besides being better educated than the stereotype
of radio fans, the FM listener was apt to be in a
higher income bracket. FM advertising picked up,
and FM receivers in cars became a status symbol.
When in 1966 the FCC ruled that FM programming
must be at least 50 per cent original (not an AM
simulcast), the affiliated stations sought a broader appeal. Commercials, popular music, live sports broadcasts, and sexy-voiced girl announcers invaded the
cloistered world of FM. Some listeners regretted it.

A second reaction was to put the "talk" part of the
music-and-news format into the driver's seat. While
people may inattentively tune in music as a background to whatever else they're doing, there can be
no such thing as "background talk." In the search for
identity, radio stations became increasingly specialized. Each talked to a specific segment of the audience. As the disc jockey had zeroed in on the teenager,
a new breed of "talkers" appealed to adults: to the
motorist, for example; or to the insomniac late at night;
to the housewife; to a particular ethnic group.

NBC's *Monitor* passed its tenth year as a weekend
talk show; the other networks followed suit. The
format features continuous news, sports, interviews,
factual features, a variety of entertainment, and some
music. During the same years RKO's station WOR
(*Radio New York*) established itself as virtually an

The WOR day began with John A. Gambling, continuing a
tradition set by his father, John Gambling, over 40 years
earlier. The program blended light-hearted conversation
with traffic and regular hourly news reports. Gambling
stayed on the air three and a half hours, seven mornings a
week, taking an occasional breather by playing records.
Except for this, most of WOR's music was relegated to commercials or to the FM affiliate.

Clowning and cornball humor had their place in the spec-
trum of radio talk. Klavan and Finch, on the air for WNEW,
New York, from 6 to 10 A.M. daily, took a zany approach
toward "demonstrating" new commercial products. Among
their most devoted followers were advertising men, who
dubbed the program "the Madison Avenue listening post."
Gene Klavan's book on his experiences was entitled *We Die
at Dawn.* Klavan and Finch traffic reports dispensed with
helicopters; they simply made loud noises with a bicycle
gadget and picked up bulletins from the police.

The completely automatic radio station became technically feasible, with taped programs put on the air complete with commercials, untouched by human hand. This is a view of control equipment at WABC, New York. A single person at this console could operate the entire station all day. CBS experimented with operating its FM affiliated stations by fully automated controls.

some provocative and acid-tongued. Whatever the mood selected, the aim was to get the listener personally involved in a subject of real (not merely theoretical) interest to himself. The ordinary person's kitchen table opinions, the barroom arguments, the bull session brainstorms gained an outlet. Radio became a forum; and often the "real" pulse of public opinion was startlingly different from the ideas of the "Establish-

all-talk station, with only occasional musical interludes. WOR hit the top in ratings with solid news coverage, interesting commentators, engaging banter such as that of the John Gamblings, father and son, and listener service. The station spent a fortune on helicopter-borne traffic spotting for motorists. All-talk stations were appearing in every metropolitan area.

Technology increased their range. With a portable tape recorder, a radio reporter can cover fast-breaking local stories for broadcast at any convenient time. He can roam the world to interview celebrated people. Taping also made possible the mechanical assemblage of high quality programs. Performers could do their turns without coming to the studio, and without regard for the clock. Radio stations began to resemble power plants, with a lone engineer commanding batteries of whirling tapes.

The telephone was another ally, used for receiving reports from the field and transferring them to tape. This led to invention of the telephone show, rage of the mid-1960's. A master of ceremonies, alone or with a featured guest, would give his phone number on the air so that listeners could get into the act. A tape delay of a few seconds protected the station from airing obscenity, libel, or drunken babble. Uninhibited radio talkers deliberately tackled "gut" issues: the more delicate and controversial, the greater the response. A test made by CBS Radio for six of its stations counted 1,070,009 busy signals—attempted phone calls to an M.C.—in a single month.

Some of the hosts were knowledgeable and friendly,

Barry Gray, an old-timer in talk radio, hosted a late show on WMCA, New York. Previously he had been a featured talker at WOR. He also had a syndicated show, aired in other cities, but his New York patter was highly show-biz oriented, ultra-liberal, and "in."

Talk radio at its best seems to need a market of major size, such as New York, Chicago, Boston, San Francisco, and one consisting of a vast assortment of populations. In Washington, a town of one industry (the U.S. Government), talking had a slow start and did not produce "personalities."

Outspoken editorializing by veteran newsman Walter Kiernan was a successful WOR feature. During the 1960's radio stations abandoned their traditional posture of strict neutrality on all public issues.

ment" as written in newspapers and magazines.

In a way, radio filled the vacuum left by the disappearance of the competitive, crusading newspaper. R. Peter Straus, president of WMCA, New York, began airing station-sponsored editorials—a revolutionary departure from radio's traditional posture of strict neutrality in "analyzing" the news. Highly opinionated talkers, some of them acerbic to the point of insult, achieved great local popularity. Not everyone greeted radio's new role with cheers. In a piece headed "Goodby Dooby-Dooby-Do, Hello Blah, Blah-Blah," *The New York Times* columnist Russell Baker wrote:

At first exposure to a few talk shows the listener thinks that radio has discovered a new comic form. The people who call in to sound off seem invariably to be the same cast. There is the angry old lady who says it's a shame about all this crime in the streets and if the police really wanted to do something about it they'd nip it in the bud by arresting those children who play in her front yard.

Serious Thinker then rings in. Things are always going too far in Serious Thinker's world. "Don't get me wrong" is his opening line. "Don't get me wrong," he says, "but this civil rights thing is going too far. . . ."

He is followed by Sports Nut. Sports Nut usually wants to tell humanity why the Giants should have gone for the yardage instead of punting on fourth down. . . .

After opening remarks by a guest, the public is urged to telephone with questions about American burial customs. Who rings in? Sports Nut. "Do you have a question

The imperishable Arthur Godfrey (right) celebrated his thirtieth anniversary with CBS Radio on January 15, 1964. Top personalities appearing with him included (left to right) concert singer Bill DuPree, raconteur Rufus Jarman, singer Richard Hayes, former Vice President Richard M. Nixon, newscaster Lowell Thomas, singer Rosemary Clooney, comedian Jackie Gleason, movie star Joan Crawford and comedian Pat Buttram. Godfrey had his ups and downs in television, but his daily radio show, *Arthur Godfrey Time*, maintained its following of millions of housewives. He thus was one of the few old-time radio stars to continue in the big time via the original medium.

Joe Pyne (left) was one of the most successful of modern-day radio talkers who used the art of insult to provoke studio guests or telephone callers into emotional outbursts that made "good copy." Those who disagree with him are apt to be called "jerk" or "meathead" or told to "Take your teeth out, put'em in backwards, and bite your throat."

Pyne has described the people's urge to brave his wrath as "a masochistic syndrome." An equally vitriolic critic, Jack Gould of *The New York Times,* called him the industry's "ranking nuisance." There was no question, though, that sharp tongue or no, Pyne and other provocative personalities had struck gold in the common people's urge to vent their logical or illogical ideas and be heard.

Tongue-in-cheek fun, with a soft, sophisticated sell, was the hallmark of Pete Myers, another of the "personality" voices counted upon to give WNEW a distinctive image. Every big city was developing local talkers as local stars—a complete reversal of the old-time network star system. Programs once listed as off-beat, such as the sophisticated Jean Shepherd on WOR in New York, developed a mass audience and spread around the country by way of syndication of their tapes to other stations.

for Doctor Thanatopsis?" "Yes, I'd like to ask the doctor what he thinks of the Cincinnati Reds trading Frank Robinson to the Orioles. . . ."

Or, after a dissertation on pie crust: . . . "Don't get me wrong, but this business of frozen pie has gone too far. It's just like the civil rights thing. You know what Abraham Lincoln really said, don't you, about how to deal with the race problem? The papers never print that, of course. Don't get me wrong now, but. . . ."

Or, "I'd just like somebody to tell me how I can get time to roll pie crust when the police won't do a thing to keep these children off my front yard."

(© 1966 by *The New York Times* Company. Reprinted by permission.)

Nevertheless, and perhaps willy-nilly, the new talkers steered radio toward an active roll in community affairs. Unlike the Arthur Godfreys of an earlier day, they made no attempt to be all things to all men

or all women, or to be merely entertaining without stepping on anyone's toes. While Godfrey himself maintained his hypnotic hold on the American housewife with light banter, the newcomers took a position.

Joe Pyne of Los Angeles, for example, was merciless toward callers who disagreed with him. Among his guests have been Black Muslims, eccentric self-styled prophets and miracle workers, American Nazis, champions of free LSD, homosexuals, and a defrocked priest. "The subject must be visceral," Pyne said. "We want emotion, not mental involvement."

In town after town, vivid personalities talked their way to local stardom, precisely the reverse of the old network star system. Some, like Pyne, were disconcerting. Some, like Bob Hall of CBS, had soothing words for folks trying to drop off to sleep; some were helpful, some informative, some iconoclastic. Some

The 21 million Negroes in America made up a $28 billion market which, advertisers discovered, preferred to listen to their own Negro radio stations. Besides music (largely by Negro artists) and other entertainment, these stations became community leaders. They considered it their function to tell what was happening in a city's Negro districts and among the Negro citizenry. The telephone "gripe" show was a popular feature, along with programs designed to help the people in contacts with the white community.

Negro stations have held "Stay in School" rallies to show the advantages of staying in school and not dropping out (WWRL, New York); have established a Goodwill Fund (WDIA, Memphis); raised money for Dr. Martin Luther King (WHAT, Philadelphia); sent reporters to Vietnam to interview Negro soldiers (WEBB, Baltimore). In Chicago, where relations with the police were strained, WBEE scheduled a weekly public service program, *BEE-line Police Beat*. Here news director Vinson J. Sanders (left) interviews police superintendent Orlando W. Wilson.

Many local radio stations subsist on remote entertaining, public service and contests. These events attract listeners and build up a devoted, loyal audience. Here, WHOM, a small station located in New York City and beamed to the Spanish speaking people of Harlem, uses these techniques successfully.

gained national rating and six-figure incomes through syndication, including Pyne and his exact opposite, ethereal Jean Shepherd of WOR. The latter, once considered strictly off-beat, gained a surprisingly large audience among the sophisticated. "Are you ready to shuffle off the mortal world of mediocrity?" he asked listeners.

Star spielers such as Murray the K ("The Fifth Beatle") and Cousin Brucie in New York were fast, witty gabbers who could change the subject within 30 seconds, considered the limit for the onset of listener boredom. Personalities came and went with bewildering rapidity, or graduated to television. On ethnic stations—those catering specifically to one ethnic group—they achieved more permanence. The civil rights movement was reflected in the growth of all-Negro and all-Spanish broadcasting as the voice of emerging minorities (an example is WVON, Chicago —Voice of the Negro).

Some 500 Negro stations in big cities and throughout the South featured the "soul sound"—a distinctive expression of rhythm and blues and gospel music. A Negro music publishing center grew up in Detroit. Spanish stations throbbed to the Latin beat in New York, Chicago, San Antonio, Miami—wherever Puerto Ricans, Mexicans, Cubans lived in *barrios* or Latin quarters. But these stations also became community leaders, taking the part of *ombudsman*, or public protector, in steering listeners through the mysteries of Anglo-Saxon mores and officialdom. In Chicago, where news director Lou House of WAAF shouts "Uhuru!" ("Freedom!") to open and close each show, the station was credited with a role in restoring order when civil rights agitation led to violence.

Marvin Kalb

Lowell Thomas

Morey Safer

On the opposite side, subsidized propaganda of the extreme right inundated the air waves, especially in rural areas. In 1966 a monitoring organization told Senate probers that 10,000 such programs a week were being supplied as tapes, free of charge, to 1,600 stations. Labeled "a major assault on American opinion," they were sponsored by right wing groups and individuals. Some cloaked politics in religious garb (*Christian Crusade, Twentieth Century Reformation Hour*). Most saw a "Red plot" everywhere, not only in acts of responsible government, but even in such trivia as folk dancing and diet cola ("a plot to weaken Americans by lowering the blood-sugar count"). Their anti-Negro, anti-Semitic, anti-Catholic, even anti-Protestant-church bias was unhappily evident.

A news magazine labeled the propaganda flood a

The importance of news to radio is indicated by the assignments of top flight newscasters by the networks to the sensitive areas of the world. Here we see Marvin Kalb at the United Nations, Lowell Thomas, just returned from a world trip, Morey Safer in South Vietnam, Roger Mudd who covers

"fourth network." The three actual networks concentrated on feeding local stations about 30 to 40 hours a week of news, information, and features that they could not produce themselves. Network celebrities continued to handle international news: NBC's Chet Huntley, CBS's Walter Cronkite, ABC's Edward P. Morgan, called "the last of the great commentators on the air." Most of these were shared with television.

Roger Mudd

Frank Kearns

Richard C. Hottelet

Eric Sevareid

Harry Reasoner

Robert Trout

the Washington scene, and Frank Kearns NBC African Correspondent. Other top newscasters include: Richard C. Hottelet (United Nations), Eric Sevareid (New York and Washington), Harry Reasoner (Washington), Robert Trout and Charles Collingwood (New York), and Douglas Edwards and Walter Cronkite (New York and Washington).

The straight news station appeared in 1961: XTRA, Tijuana, Mexico, a licensee serving the Los Angeles area. It provided news like a telephone service, 24 hours a day, whenever the listener chose to tune in. Other stations adopted the plan, notably WNUS, Chicago (pronounced "W-News") and WINS, New York, rock 'n' roll headquarters before payola.

Election coverage entered a new, some thought dangerous, phase with "instant prediction." In 1964 and 1966, computers fed with early voting samples predicted the results with uncanny speed. Often the networks announced a "winner" before there had been any official count at all. Although sometimes they were wrong, they were right often enough to create a "bandwagon" psychology in the West. Because of the difference in time, a California voter knew who had won in the East before he had voted himself. To prevent this, Frank Stanton of CBS and Elmer Lower of ABC proposed a nationwide, 24-hour, uniform polling period. Thereby no sample precincts could be counted until all polls had closed.

Popular music on the radio sought a quieter sound, even though teenagers continued to breed heroes like the "Geator With the Heater" (Jerry Blavat) in Phila-

Charles Collingwood

Douglas Edwards

Walter Cronkite

The Barry Gray Show on WMCA, New York, is an example of serious radio journalism in the "talk" format. Here, Barry Gray (third from left) moderates a discussion during the 1965 mayoralty race between Democrat Abraham Beame (second from right), Conservative William C. Buckley (extreme right) and Liberal-Republican John V. Lindsay (extreme left), who was elected.

dephia. College students embraced folk music, making stars of Joan Baez, Bob Dylan, Peter, Paul, and Mary. The blue-collar, adult, working class, made country music supreme in following. This was a blend of Southern ("hillbilly") balladry with a Western roll, a "rock" beat, twangy electric guitars, and the most forlorn lyrics ever sung. Nashville, Tennessee, home of *Grand Ole Opry*, became second only to New York as a music recording center.

In the new found prosperity, radio stations increased in number from 4,250 in 1960 to 5,280 in 1965, more than eight times the 704 television stations. Advertising revenue, which had slumped 50 per cent in the 1950's, jumped $330 million in ten years, pushing close to $1 billion at mid-decade. A large part was accounted for by spot commercials.

The Big Three automobile makers spent $41 million on spot radio in 1965, a 16 per cent gain in one year. Tobacco, soft drinks, beer, gasoline, and toiletries were other top sponsors, reflecting the adult male audience in cars. But soaps and cosmetics were returning to the fold, too; and CBS announced a new program specifically devoted to women drivers.

As a creative medium, radio seemed unable to match the visual techniques of television. Contemporary drama was limited to a few productions such as ABC's *Theatre Five*, and to local FM stations such as WRVR, the voice of Riverside Church in New York. Some of the old serials, however, were successfully revived, including *The Shadow, The Green Hornet*, and the "Hi-yo, Silver!" of *The Lone Ranger*. A radio show has the special quality of forcing the listener to use his imagination, making the characters and situations all the more memorable.

Commercial radio contributed two leading newscasters to the Government. Edward R. Murrow resigned as vice president of CBS to become head of the United States Information Agency. His new career was cut short by his early death from lung cancer. Later, NBC's John Chancellor took over *Voice of America*, which broadcasts 800 hours a week in 38 languages, including Swahili, to every corner of the globe. In essence, he adopted the successful *Monitor* format to make Uncle Sam's political propaganda more attractive to the listener.

In the 1960's, radio performed best as a news medium, bringing events directly into the home . . . quickly, accurately and dramatically. And because of its comparatively low cost operation, radio provided news service continuously, wherever and whenever it became necessary (a difficult task for television). These photographs show CBS Radio coverage of the 1960 Democratic (right) and Republican (above) National Conventions.

The "Number One Cat" of Philadelphia in 1966 was 24-year-old Jerry Blavat, the "Geator with the Heater," the "Boss with the Hot Sauce." He was representative of a special type of disc jockey, often on a small station (WCAM, Camden, N.J., 1,000 watts), who totally captivated local teen-agers and headed for the big time. "Geator" (Alligator) Blavat received $28 a week from radio, but about $135,000 a year from personal appearances at record hops, albums, and a TV show. Nationally known Dick Clark, Lloyd Thaxton, and Murray the K had a similar beginning.

Country music, also known as C&W (country and Western), rockabilly, or the "Nashville Sound," spread from the South to become the "new sound" of some 1,500 local radio stations in big cities as well as rural areas.

Actually there was nothing new about country music, which had been on the air longer than any other kind except classical music. A succession of modern performers, however, had eliminated the raw "hillbilly" twang and added a strong beat derived from rock 'n' roll. Smooth "sweet" singers, and sidemen adept at improvising a bass with steel guitars and a ring-a-ling rhythm, added the urbanity it needed. In 1965 country music accounted for 25 per cent of all popular record releases and $70 million, about 10 per cent of total record sales in America.

The music comes from the working class. The melodies are tuneful, the rhythms simple, and the lyrics are close to the heart. They reflect the daily lives of the common people who love, hate, win, or lose. Some typical hit titles: *Divorce Me, C.O.D., It Wasn't God Who Made Honky-Tonk Angels, I'm Throwing Rice at the Girl I Love, Dear John Letter, Why Don't You Haul Off and Love Me?, I Don't Hurt Anymore, I've Enjoyed As Much of This as I Can Stand.*

A Country Music Hall of Fame and Museum was opened in Nashville, home of a $60 million annual business in recordings, in 1966. Among the immortals in the genre have been Jimmie Rodgers (*I'm in the Jailhouse Now*), Hank Williams (*Hey, Good Lookin', Your Cheatin' Heart*), Roger Miller (*King of the Road*), Ernest Tubb, Eddy Arnold (*Anytime*), Roy Acuff, Tex Ritter, and Fred Rose.

Singer Ray Price (right) finds himself in a sea of autograph hunters at a live show sponsored by WBMB, Baltimore, at the Civic Center. Crowds for live country-and-Western shows (left) have ranged as high as 33,000. They and the record sales have made wealthy men (and women) of performers and composers once considered in the "barefoot" class.

A nostalgic reunion on the Chase and Sanborn show in 1966 brought together Edgar Bergen and Charlie McCarthy with former members of the *Allen's Alley* cast, in a salute to the late Fred Allen. They are Minerva Pious (Mrs. Nussbaum), Kenny Delmar (Senator Claghorn), and Peter Donald (Ajax Cassidy).

Radio technology played a sensational role in the exploration of outer space. In alliance with the computer and automated mechanisms, radio signals guided unmanned vehicles through hundreds of millions of miles to Mars and Venus—a feat considered pure fantasy only a few years before. The voices of astronaut John Glenn and his successors, from capsules orbiting

in space, could be heard by millions of earthbound listeners. Astonishing closeup photographs of the Moon and planets were flashed home by a sophisticated form of radio facsimile. Direct broadcasts from human explorers of the Moon are confidently expected.

The Telstar satellite inaugurated commercial transmission of sight and sound signals across the oceans and continents. Microelectronics—an integrated circuit in a silicon chip smaller than a pinhead—made the transistor look gigantic. Scientists forecast a time when everyone would carry a chip-circuit radio in his wrist-watch or hatband, with a calling number for instant communication with any other person anywhere on earth.

In the 1960's, saturation mass communication by radio became a fact of modern life. The added income from radio's universal audience meant better programming, more thoughtful interpretation and commentary, added services of all kinds to the listener.

Martin Block, inventor of *Make Believe Ballroom* in 1935 and dean of disc jockeys, was one of the few musical features remaining in WOR all-talk programming. He continued to play records and comment breezily between them on Saturday and Sunday mornings. Block's longevity in a changing industry testified to the basic appeal of exciting the listener's imagination—in his case by creating the illusion that the recorded bands were playing for him "live." This element of romantic mystery is lacking in television.

The 30-year-old *Make Believe Ballroom,* now in the hands of William B. Williams at WNEW, became part of the "Broadway beat" for visiting show people. Here Frank Sinatra drops in for a bit of banter to open the proceedings. The husky-voiced Williams steered Ballroom away from "rock" toward a higher grade of popular music. He said, "I have a theory you could take one group of rock 'n' roll guys, introduce them as the Nosebleeds or some such, rush them off stage, put wigs on them and rush them back as the Earaches. The kids would never know.

# Index